T0271558

THE POWER OF
MANIFESTING

About the Authors

Anne Jirsch is a psychic, tarot consultant, metaphysical teacher, radio and newspaper astrologer, past life regressionist and future life progressionist. Her client base includes heads of industry, politicians and celebrities from the world of film, media, show business and sport. She is the author of *Instant Intuition* and *The Future is Yours*.

Monica Cafferky is an author, yoga teacher and journalist who has written for numerous publications, including the *Daily Mirror*, *Daily Express*, *Red*, *Grazia* and *Woman's Own*. In 1997, Monica won a scholarship to attend a training course at Green College, Oxford with Reuters. She is now a Fellow of the Thomson Reuters Foundation. Her debut novel, *The Winter's Sleep*, won praise from Fay Weldon, who described it as 'thought-provoking and very human'. Monica is also the co-author of *Instant Intuition* and *The Future is Yours*.

THE POWER OF MANIFESTING

How to harness
cosmic energy to
transform your life

ANNE JIRSCH
AND
MONICA CAFFERKY

PIATKUS

PIATKUS

First published in Great Britain in 2009 by Piatkus
This paperback edition published in 2024 by Piatkus

1 3 5 7 9 10 8 6 4 2

Copyright © 2009 by Anne Jirsch and Monica Cafferky

A CIP catalogue record for this book
is available from the British Library.

ISBN 978-0-3494-3943-3

Printed and bound in Great Britain by
Clays Ltd, Elcograf S.p.A.

Papers used by Piatkus are from well-managed forests
and other responsible sources.

Piatkus
An imprint of
Little, Brown Book Group
Carmelite House
50 Victoria Embankment
London EC4Y 0DZ

An Hachette UK Company
www.hachette.co.uk

www.littlebrown.co.uk

For Dan

To see a world in a grain of sand
And heaven in a wild flower
Hold infinity in the palm of your hand
and eternity in an hour

From 'Auguries of Innocence', William Blake

Contents

Acknowledgements

I would like to say a special thanks to Paul McKenna, as without you I would not be where I am today. Paul Duddridge: your advice has been invaluable. To Judy Piatkus, for giving me such a wonderful break; Robert Kirby, the best agent a girl can have, and Monica Cafferky, for surviving working on all three books with me.

Also, the following people need a special thank you for permission granted to quote from their work or for giving time for interviews: Antonietta Breinza, John Solagbade, Ben Harrington, Seka Nikolic, Tony James, Tony Ford, Graham James, Carmen Clews, Clare Staples, Kevin Laye, Rita Gerathy, Professor Richard Wiseman, Woody Hochswender, Greg Martin and Ted Morino; and to the following living geniuses whose work is truly ahead of its time: Dr Richard Bandler and Dr Roger Callahan.

Foreword

By Paul McKenna

Often when people talk about energy they are referring to a feeling of motivation, of 'get up and go'!

However, energy is much more than that. I have a friend who has extraordinary good luck in life. He is rich in every sense and people love spending time with him, in fact someone once said to me, 'If he could bottle and sell his energy everyone would want it.'

But what is energy?

Our whole lives are about our energy. The entire universe in fact is energy because, as Einstein demonstrated with his famous formula $E=mc^2$, matter and energy are just different forms of the same thing.

A human being is a mass of energy vibrating at different frequencies. All of your thoughts and feelings affect your energy, which in turn affects your behaviours, your impact on other people and the results you get in life.

I was very sceptical about anything of a metaphysical nature until I presented a TV series where we investigated the paranormal. After having seen so many things that cannot be explained by conventional science I now keep a very open mind.

In this fascinating book Anne explores some of the scientific findings and the metaphysical ideas about how we can use this extraordinary invisible force that affects every aspect of our lives. She has taken some rather complicated and abstract ideas and turned them into user-friendly concepts and techniques.

If you would like to know how to fill yourself with positive energy and send that energy out in to the world, the exercises in this book will help you do just that.

The results will be life changing!

Paul McKenna

CHAPTER 1

Working with Cosmic Energy

You are energy. Everything you see, smell, taste or touch is energy. Every plant, tree, creature, object – even your thoughts and feelings – are energy. Even where there appears to be nothing, in what seems like empty space, there is energy. Everything in the universe and beyond is made up of what I like to call Cosmic Energy, or chi, the 'universal force'.

Once you accept that Cosmic Energy really exists, that it is all around you and that it impacts upon you every day, you can work with it in all situations to improve your life.

Some people seem to be naturally attuned to their Cosmic Energy. You know the kind – those lucky ones who always fall on their feet. Life seems easier for them and they always seem to get what they want; they attract positive people into their lives and find themselves in really fortunate situations, in the right place at the right time. Even when they experience disaster, they come up smelling of roses! How do they manage to always turn things around? Are they born lucky?

The answer to this question is simple. Whether they know it or not, these 'charmed' people are attuned to their Cosmic Energy. This gives them a direct link to the universe and an aspect of control over their lives that the majority of people don't have because they are not working with the universal chi.

In this book I will teach you how to connect with Cosmic Energy and show you how to work with this power in all situations to harmonise your own life. I am going to help you become one of the charmed ones – and boost your manifesting skills.

You will learn how to:

◆ Attract positive people into your life

◆ Raise your love vibration to attract your soul mate and a wonderful love life

◆ Create wealth and abundance

◆ Succeed in business and stay ahead of your competitors

◆ Create your own perfect healing space to clear stress, create balance and restore and energise your entire being

◆ Make a great impression on people and leave a little of your own energy behind so they remember you

You will also learn how you can achieve your full potential and happiness in this incarnation and how to connect with your Higher Self. Your Higher Self is your soul, the eternal being connected to the universal life force. Every time we incarnate in a physical body, the Higher Self tries to help us to achieve our goals and aims for this lifetime with subtle nudges through dreams, activating our intuition and making us aware of coincidences that point us in the right direction. We agree to these life goals with our spirit guides before we incarnate and when we pass over from this life, this particular soul experience, what we have learnt is absorbed back into our Higher Self – which in turn contains all experiences from all lifetimes.

I believe that every single one of us has various goals we wish to achieve in this incarnation, but life is hard and sometimes the hurdles thrown in our way trip us up. By connecting to Cosmic Energy you can access a way to remove the difficulties that cause most people to stumble. I am not saying that I can give you a magic wand, but what I can do is show you how to become one of those lucky people who are in the right place at the right time, who are able to make the most of every situation and who utilise the power all around them – the power of Cosmic Energy.

My Own Experience with Cosmic Energy

I have worked for over thirty years in the spiritual field as a psychic, tarot consultant, past life regressionist and future life progressionist (where you go into the future using deep hypnosis and relaxation techniques). During my work with past life regression, I have taken a great many people back into their past lives and, while doing so, have often been amazed at how in tune our ancient selves were with the energy of the universe. They understood it, they lived in accordance with the seasons; and they inherently knew how to use Cosmic Energy to their benefit.

Today we are living in a time of great technological advances. We have satellites in space; we use mobile phones, email, the iPhone, sat-navs and other amazing tools without a second thought. Sadly, though, most people have forgotten how to experience life without machines and how to trust their instincts; how to respond to and work with the energy that surrounds them. Likewise, we have made great medical advances in the development of manufactured drugs, but at one time we knew how to heal ourselves using our own energy.

The majority of people work so hard to build a decent life,

they struggle and suffer day in, day out. Yet we once knew how to attract everything we needed, just by using the power of the mind and the energy of the earth.

Vikram and Greta

I have been lucky; over the years I have had a number of mentors cross my path who have taught me a great deal. During my time in India I met Vikram, a beggar who lived on the streets of Calcutta. He was one of the happiest men I have ever met, despite his circumstances. He was loved by people and seemed to have an endless source of wisdom. Each day I would drop in to see him and ask him questions about everything under the sun.

Vikram would tell me, 'The things you worry about are not important. What is important is that you are a being of energy that has been around in one form or another since time began.' At the time it was hard to understand that we are not just flesh and bones. One day I asked him, 'How do you know all this new stuff?' In the early 1970s when people in the West first heard of Eastern spirituality, everyone thought they were discovering something new and exciting.

He laughed and replied, 'This knowledge is as old as time. There is nothing I tell you that you do not already know and hasn't been known forever, which is why it doesn't matter whether I sit in a mansion or on my mat here, because when you realise you are energy, nothing else matters. You move beyond the material.'

At the time, I had no idea how important his words would become decades later.

On my return from India I was drawn to a healer and counsellor by the name of Greta Gill. She was a remarkable woman who had a subtle way of teaching. Every so often she would point out something I had said or an undercurrent of events that had gone unnoticed by others. She explained that if I felt I was on the same wavelength as someone else or that another person was giving me bad vibes, or a place gave me the creeps, that it was just to do with people sending out their energy, which would then affect my personal vibrations.

Greta told me, 'When you meet someone you dislike for no apparent reason, or go to a place that feels uncomfortable, you feel their energy and it can leave an imprint.' How often have your walked into a house or building and thought, 'Oh, I don't like this place'? When this happens you are picking up on the energy, you are using your instinct. What I hope to teach you throughout this book is how to connect with your own vibration, or energy, and that of other people and your environment. This is how you can begin to work with Cosmic Energy.

The Etheric Energy Technique

All those years ago, I didn't understand Vikram or Greta's messages, but they did open my mind so that at a later date things fell into place, and once I began to realise the importance of energy it gave my life a whole new dimension. As I began to work with Tarot I knew that energy played a part – it gave me answers and connected me to my clients.

But somehow I knew there was more. Fifteen years ago I began to have dreams about our energy fields, which led me to develop the Etheric Energy Technique (EET). This is a wonderful way to use your own energy field to have an out-of-body experience, send telepathic messages and even leave a strong impression on a person or place. You will find many new exciting Etheric Energy techniques throughout this book.

In my first book, *Instant Intuition*, I mentioned Alladale, a mystical wilderness in Scotland owned by Paul Lister (which later became the focus of a BBC 2 documentary series *The Real Monarch of the Glen*). During one Christmas visit to Alladale in 2006 I had what I would call an enlightenment moment – a spiritual epiphany –a major step forward in my understanding of Cosmic Energy and how the universe works. This is what happened to me during my life-changing visit to this mystical place.

On a bitterly cold morning, the estate rangers had driven my party to the top of the mountain on this vast estate to take part in a deer hunt; the animals were culled to keep the balance at Alladale. As I am not the hardiest of people, I decided to stay near the jeep and let the others hunt.

After everyone disappeared I stood on top of this beautiful mountain utterly alone and I sensed total peace. At that moment I felt as if I was the only being in the universe.

I have been high up in mountains before – I've travelled over the Khyber Pass, across a mountain in Iran and stood among the clouds in Chihuahua, Mexico – but the remoteness at Alladale is different. You can feel the pure, untainted energy all around you. Yet as I stood there, I also felt connected to the earth and the earth felt like part of me. I breathed in, and energised every cell of my body. I became aware of the sky above me and I felt connected to the sky and to the universe. It was the purest energy I had ever experienced. My thoughts became clear and at that moment nothing could worry me. I gained a great feeling of peace.

I suddenly felt as if I truly understood how we could be connected to absolutely everything and everyone in the universe. I had always struggled to understand quantum physics and how everything is linked, but now I fully realised the awesome energy that surrounds us, which we can tap into and use at will.

I grasped that because we are part of everything, if we criticise something we criticise ourselves; if we are bad to someone or something, we are in turn bad to ourselves. I realised that this was the true meaning of karma. I also realised that unconsciously we choose what we attract and that we can control our energy to create what we want. By using Cosmic Energy, we can control our own reality. To me, that revelation was the most important part of the message.

Science and Spirituality: Getting the Connection
For hundreds of years, theories such as Darwinism have challenged the existence of God, suggesting that there may be no great power overseeing the workings of the universe, no life after death, or cosmic force which connects us with an invisible undercurrent, creating our reality. Yet now, science and spirituality are beginning to meet in the middle.

The Hundredth Monkey
One study that changed modern-day thinking took place in 1958 on the Japanese island of Koshima. The results coined the term 'non-locality', which means 'things that appear not to be connected can affect one other'. This amazing study was to become the basis of the famous book *The Hundredth Monkey Effect* by Ken Keyes, Jr.

The researchers were monitoring a group of macaque monkeys and observed that some had learnt to wash sweet potatoes. As you would expect, the younger monkeys began to copy them. The odd thing was the scientists noticed that once a critical number of monkeys had learnt this skill (known as the hundredth monkey) the skill instantly spread across the water to monkeys on nearby islands – even though they had no contact with each other, and could not see what the original monkeys were doing. This study shows that what we do affects others, and begins to explain things such as when people on opposite sides of the world suddenly come up with the same idea at the same time, such as a medical breakthrough or an idea for a movie.

Scientist Dean Radin, in his book *Entangled Minds,* states, 'Non locality means that there are ways in which things that appear to be separate are, in fact, not separate.'

The truth is that the more separate we feel, the harder life is – which is why it's so important to be aligned to Cosmic Energy and feel connected not only to the universal chi but to the planet, animals and other beings. Once we feel the connection to all things, life becomes a lot easier.

Biologist Rupert Sheldrake, who has conducted a vast number of studies into telepathy, suggests in his book *The Sense of Being Stared At* that we create fields of perception that stretch around us, connecting us to what we are looking at. Through these fields, the observer and the observed are interconnected. He believes our minds reach out beyond our brains and into the world around us. He says, 'Your brain is within the confines of your cranium. Your mind is extended into space, and stretches out into the world around you. It reaches out to touch what you see. If you look at a mountain ten miles away, your mind is stretching out ten miles. If you look at a distant star, your mind is extending over literally astronomical distances.' Once we realise that we can connect to people, things and places, we begin to realise that we can also affect these things. We have the ability to take control and to use this power, this Cosmic Energy, to change our lives for the better.

Can Water Remember?

One of the most groundbreaking pieces of research on energy in recent years has been that of Masaru Emoto's study with water crystals (see Appendix). Emoto, a Japanese researcher, began looking into homeopathy, whereby a medicine is diluted in water until the medicine is no longer detectable. The diluted medicine eventually has no trace of the original medicine, yet even without any trace at all has the same curative effect as the original medicine.

Emoto decided to study this concept further to see if somehow water could 'remember'. He began to freeze water and take photographs of the crystals that were formed – with astonishing results. At first, Emoto looked at the crystals formed from samples of tap water taken from different locations. He could not find one crystal in his frozen sample of heavily chlorinated water from Tokyo, yet natural spring water, no matter where it was from, always formed beautiful, complete crystals.

He then decided to see what would happen if he played music to the water, then froze it to form crystals. Again, he was sure the music would somehow affect the water. Placing a bottle of water on a table with two speakers either side, music was played to the water – and again, the results were astonishing. When frozen, water that had been played classical musical made beautiful, well-formed crystals, but water that had been played heavy metal music formed distorted and malformed frozen crystals.

Next, he took things further. Emoto wrote words onto pieces of paper like 'fool' and 'thank you'. It sounded crazy to think that the water could somehow read the words, but if words carried an energy and water was the best absorber of energy, then maybe something interesting would happen. The water receiving the words 'thank you' formed wonderful crystals, but the water receiving the word 'fool' made similar distorted shapes as the liquid exposed to the heavy metal music. The most beautiful frozen crystals were formed by water that had been exposed to the words 'love' and 'gratitude'.

If our bodies are 70 per cent water and words carry a vibration that affects water, it stands to reason that words greatly affect us.

> 'The entire universe is in a state of vibration, and each thing generates its own frequency, which is unique.'
>
> Masaru Emoto

Thoughts Create Reality

More and more eminent scientists are suggesting that what we think affects our reality. One scientist, Professor Richard Wiseman, a psychologist at the University of Hertfordshire and a CSICOP fellow (the Committee for the Scientific Investigation of Claims of the Paranormal), wanted to find the answers to questions we often have about luck: can we create our own luck? Why do some people lead lives filled with repeated failure and sadness while others enjoy happy successful existence? Why do some stagger from one broken relationship to the next, while others find their perfect partner? What enables some people to have successful careers while apparently similar others find themselves trapped in dead-end jobs they detest? And most importantly, can unlucky people do anything to improve their luck – and unhappy lives? Professor Wiseman spent ten years studying people's attitudes to luck and chance and how this affected their reality. His revolutionary study of luck and its power to transform people's lives is now a best-selling book *The Luck Factor*, which has been published in over twenty-five countries.

The Luck Experiment

Professor Wiseman decided to search for the elusive luck factor by investigating the actual beliefs and experiences of lucky and unlucky people. He says:

Over the years, four hundred extraordinary men and women have volunteered to participate in my research; the youngest eighteen, a student, the oldest eighty-four, a retired accountant. They were drawn from all walks of life and all were kind enough to let me put their lives and minds under the microscope.

The differences between the lucky and unlucky people were striking. Lucky people tend to imagine spontaneously how the bad luck they encounter could have been worse and, in doing so, they feel much better about themselves and their lives. This, in turn, helps keep their expectations about the future high, and increases the likelihood of them continuing to live a lucky life.

I wondered whether the principles uncovered during my work could be used to increase the amount of good luck that people encounter in their lives. To find out, I created 'luck school' – a series of experiments examining whether people's luck can be enhanced by getting them to think and behave like a lucky person. The project comprised two main parts. In the first part I met up with participants on a one-to-one basis, and asked them to complete standard questionnaires measuring their luck and how satisfied they were with six major areas of their life. I then described the four main principles of luck, explained how lucky people used these to create good fortune in their lives, and described simple techniques designed to help them think and behave like a lucky person.

For example, without realizing it, lucky people tend to use various techniques to create chance opportunities that surround them and deal more effectively with bad luck by imagining how things could have been worse. I asked my volunteers to spend a month carrying out exercises and then return and describe what had happened. The results were dramatic. Eighty per cent of people were now happier, more satisfied with their lives, and, perhaps most important of all, luckier. Unlucky people had become lucky, and lucky people had become even luckier. After a few weeks carrying out some simple exercises, bad luck completely vanished for many of the participants. Other volunteers found romantic partners through chance and job promotions simply through lucky breaks.

After ten years of scientific research my work has revealed a radically new way of looking at luck and the vital role it plays in our lives. It demonstrates that much of the good and bad fortune we encounter is a result of our thoughts and behavior. More important, it represents the potential for change, and has produced that most elusive of holy grails – an effective way of increasing the luck people experience in their daily lives.

Here are Professor Wiseman's four top tips for becoming lucky:

1. Listen to your gut instincts – they are normally right.

2. Be open to new experiences and breaking your normal routine.

3. Spend a few moments each day remembering things that went well.

4. Visualise yourself being lucky before an important meeting or telephone call.

And remember, luck is very often a self-fulfilling prophecy.

Positive Thinking

In my opinion, Professor Wiseman's research highlighted some fascinating facts. While he would describe himself as a sceptic (regarding psychic matters), his study demonstrates that by taking a different attitude people who previously had been unlucky in life began to create the world they wanted – they could become lucky.

I believe that by taking that positive attitude, the participants gave their dreams a new energy and vigour. In other words, by thinking that they were more lucky, they expected to be luckier and that expectation had an energy which created their luck. This chain reaction is known as the Law of Attraction: what we focus on occurs. Yet there is nothing new about the Law of Attraction, cosmic ordering or manifesting. Many ancient texts such as the Bible state, 'As you reap so shall ye sow.' Buddha said, 'All that we are is the result of what we have thought. The mind is everything. What we think we become.' In Hinduism, one of the main concepts is the law of karma: what you give out, you get back. And if you live and think positively a better life will flow your way.

In recent times we have seen a flurry of books on cosmic ordering and the Law of Attraction, yet this trend was emerging in the early twentieth century. Dale Carnegie in his 1936 book *How to Win Friends and Influence People* promoted the idea that if you wanted to get on in life then you should think positively, because your actions and thoughts created your reality. He believed that when you saw the good in people suddenly everyone would be on your side and help you to achieve your goals. In this worldwide best-seller he cited a number of case studies in which employers had a high turnover of staff and also believed that their workers were lazy. Yet after the bosses adjusted their thinking and treated their staff better, suddenly they became the perfect employees. James Allen, in his 1902 book *As Man Thinketh*, states, 'Of all the beautiful truths pertaining to the soul that have been restored and brought to light in this age, none is more gladdening or fruitful of divine promise and confidence than this – that you are the master of your thought, the moulder of your character, and the maker and shaper of your condition, environment and destiny.' The main message here is what you focus on you create, so if you focus on making money or attracting love into your life, that is what will flow your way. However, if your thoughts are more inclined towards, 'Nothing good ever happens to me,' or 'I am unlucky in love/ money/ work/ friends' then this negativity is what you will attract.

The problem is that for the vast majority of people it's very difficult to keep their thoughts 100 per cent positive all the time, especially if their past thought process has been the absolute opposite. Most people put in their cosmic order or write down their list of wants and happily send it off to the universe but at some point begin to think, 'I bet I don't get it.' Or, 'But if I get the acting job/new man, after a while they may reject me or I will make a mistake.' In other words, doubts creep in and send a completely different message to the universe. As Stuart Wilde puts it in *The Trick to Money is Having Some*: 'Now think about the Universal Law. It reflects to you exactly and precisely what you put out. If your thought forms say, "I haven't got a clue about what I want", the Universal Law is going to say, "Listen, mate, if you haven't a clue, neither have I".'

Cosmic Energy is the powerful universal force that is all around you, it connects you to your environment, people, animals and, like an unseen pulsing web, creates and controls your reality. By drawing in this Cosmic Energy you give your desire power and strength. You make it more real and concrete, and create intensity and focus. Graham James, master magician, once said, 'All magic is finding the right tools to aid your own focus.'

The Spiritual Rules for Working with Cosmic Energy

1. Always open up and close down after each exercise to make sure that you draw in only pure Cosmic Energy (see pages 23, 24)

2. Be clear about what you want to achieve.

3. As you begin to get what you want, help others get what they want – this unselfish action helps the universal energy to flow. Americans call it 'Paying it Forward' (PIF) – and there is also a Paying It Forward Movement which sprang up following the novel of the same name by Catherine Ryan Hyde (see www.payitforwardmovement.org).

4. Always show gratitude. When something good happens you

may want to look upwards towards the universe and say 'thank you'. You may wish to acknowledge the benefit in some other way, or maybe pass some goodness on to someone else with an act of kindness.

5. Have faith that whatever happens will be for your own better good.

How to Use this Book

When you read biographies of people who have achieved outstanding success, they have had no doubts whatsoever that they would succeed. They let nothing stand in their way. They can have thousands of people tell them they will never get anywhere, yet they keep going and have complete faith. They always get what they want – because they are 100 per cent unflinching and focused on their goal, they draw in Cosmic Energy; everyone else needs a bit of help. As you work through this book, decide what you want to achieve the most and focus on this area first before moving on to other areas in your life that you would like to improve.

In the following pages you will learn many never-seen-before techniques. Some will work better for you than others – but the key to Cosmic Energy is to work with what suits you best. You may be a visual person and, if so, then working with imagery will be good for you, such as following the visualisations and meditations on pages 25–6, 94. If you are more studious, keeping a log and writing things down may be more beneficial (see page 18). If you are a 'hands-on' type of person, then for you using the energy sprays and practical exercises will work well.

As well as playing to your own strengths, do also use a combination of tools and techniques, because this produces a really powerful energy.

Each exercise in this book has been carefully put together to create a powerful effect. Take your time working your way through the book, allowing each exercise to create the energy you require.

Here's what you will discover in the following chapters:

◆ In Chapter 2 are the tools and techniques that we will be using throughout the book. I have gathered these through trial and error and by studying our ancient selves – they knew how to work with the earth, the universe, the planets and the seasons.

◆ In Chapter 3 we look at love and relationships, and how love flows easily to some and not to others. We will explore how to clear problems that block your flow of love and learn how to raise your own love vibration, how to communicate with partners who are difficult to talk to and how to create the perfect love nest.

◆ Chapter 4 guides you to attune to your Cosmic Energy to attract wealth and create a flow of abundance.

◆ Chapter 5 covers the all-important topic of work and how to find your true vocation. Use your energy to create an impression at interviews and auditions, connect with your boss and colleagues or create the perfect workspace.

◆ Chapter 6 explores your Life Purpose. All that you need to know is already within you – learn how to use the tools and techniques in Chapter 2 to help you access that information.

How coincidences are guiding you every moment of your life.

◆ Chapter 7 looks at your connection to the earth, the universe and to others. You will discover how everything you think and do echoes back to you. I reveal transforming tools that allow your mind, body and sprit to align and connect to the universal force.

Come with me to discover and use the amazing energy tools that will create the life you have dreamed of – and the life you deserve.

··

Creating a Cosmic Energy Journal

As you work your way through the book it is a good idea to keep a Cosmic Energy Journal. This will help you to discover what combination of tools work best for you. You may find some tools and exercises work better with some areas of your life and a different set work better in other areas. By keeping a journal you will have a log for future reference.

In your journal, make a note of:

◆ The date

◆ The technique you used and why you used it

◆ The combination of tools you used

◆ The result

As you find the combinations of tools that work for you, you will be able to use them over and over, putting you firmly in control of your life and your destiny.

CHAPTER 2
Your Cosmic Energy Tool Kit

I have been working with past lives for over 20 years. During this period I have been continually fascinated by how our ancient selves were aware of energy; how we worked with the phases of the moon and the seasons. We understood nature and looked to the stars and planets and understood their effects on us and our environment. The Cosmic Energy Tools that I introduce to you on pages 24–54 will help you rediscover what came naturally to our ancestors – a way to alter reality by working with the energy that surrounds you.

Ancient Energy Wisdom

Today, a few cultures still have that knowledge and understanding of energy. Aboriginal people see telepathy as a part of everyday life, sending messages to each other over great distances, they have no doubt that the message will be received. They also have out-of-body experiences, travelling to distant places – this is a normal part of their existence. Native Americans also understand the earth's energy and know how to work with it instead of against it. They understand that life has a natural rhythm and by flowing with this rhythm we become in synch, life becomes easier and things are how they should be – simple, straightforward and abundant.

Both Aboriginal and Native American people work with energy for specific ends. For example, Aboriginal people use a similar migratory instinct to that of birds; they build energy between themselves and the object or place they wish to connect with, a process known as 'psi-tracking'. Psi-tracks are like invisible paths, used by Aborigines to travel from one place to another. The travellers focus on their path and sing songs to strengthen the connection. Later, other people may find their way onto the same psi-track by singing the same song, which somehow holds the message or energy. Cassandra Eason in her book *Pendulum Dowsing* shows that dowsers can also find this energy, these psi-tracks. The Swede Göte Andersson even believes psi-tracks are how seafarers of old found their way across oceans on starless nights.

During the rain dance, Native Americans go into an altered state and use the power of chant, song and dance to influence the weather. Their songs carry an energy that they believe connects them to the universe, sending a request for the rain that is needed to ensure their harvest. They also believe their dancing can influence the weather by changing the energy of the environment. The rain dance, therefore, was an early form of manifesting.

Native Americans see the earth as a living organism, which they live upon and must respect. They communicate with the earth and feel its vibration. Joseph Rael (Beautiful Painted Arrow), a mystic of Pueblo and an Ute Indian, says, 'I came to understand that the earth has always been talking to us, but many of us have lost our sensitivities to sound and to vibration, so we do not hear her. Through sound she is telling us exactly what is going to happen next, but we haven't been able to hear her because we have lost our sensitivity to work as worship. We have forgotten how to listen to what our efforts have been saying.'

It's almost impossible to measure scientifically the success of energy work like psi-tracks or a rain dance. But as you learnt in the opening chapter, Japanese researcher Masaru Emoto has been working on the power of thought – and the results of his studies are amazing. As you now know, Emoto's premise is that thoughts can change the structure of water, and so it follows that thoughts can also have an impact on a person and an environment. As I am always telling my clients, 'Thoughts are things', and thought in the form of visualisation, or affirmations, is just one of the many tools I'm going to teach you in this chapter. You will also learn about the tools for working with Cosmic Energy, what they are and how to use them. I have also included basic exercises to introduce some of the techniques and give you a taster of how to work with them.

Before You Begin: Opening Up and Closing Down

But before I go any further, I want to talk to you about a very important part of any spiritual technique – opening up and closing down. Opening up before you begin any spiritual exercise allows you to tap into your intuition and link in with Cosmic Energy. When you have finished the exercise, make sure you close down. Closing down puts you in control of your energy, so that the energy of others cannot affect you without your knowledge. By closing down you will not be so susceptible to the negative emotions of people and places.

Closing down after doing an exercise also keeps you grounded. You don't know what I mean by being grounded? Have you ever heard the Irish phrase, 'Away with the fairies?' Met people who have that permanent dreamy look in their eyes? Or, perhaps you know someone who believes everything they read and hear in the spiritual field without questioning it or using their intuition to tell them if it feels right. These people are not grounded, and being grounded in reality is a good thing – after all, we are all here to experience this reality, are we not? Being grounded allows you to step back from the spiritual world, and spiritual work, into your normal life and society. Before you begin any of the exercises, I also advise that you practise opening up and closing down. It's a good discipline, and you can try it anywhere, any time. Throughout the book I will advise when you need to open up and close down. If you have been practising it will feel easy and natural to you.

Opening Up

1. Sit or stand and allow your body to loosen. Feel the muscles around your eyes and mouth relax, and allow yourself a slight smile. Feel your shoulders coming down and any tension in your back or neck easing. Now feel the relaxing feeling flowing up and down your body.

2. Allow your breathing to deepen and become even, flowing comfortably. When any thoughts come into your mind, just allow them to float away for this short time. You do not need them just now.

3. Now imagine a beautiful white light shining down from the universe. It flows right into the top of your head, flowing down and connecting you with the universal energy that knows everything. Feel the energy connect you, and allow your own energy to flow easily and naturally.

....

Closing Down

1. After each exercise allow your breathing to become regular and feel the white light slowly drawing back towards the universe. It has now completed its job.

2. Allow your own energy – your aura and Etheric Energy – come back to its usual size and shape. Know that each time you use your energy and tap into the universal force the connection has become a little stronger, protecting you and keeping you aware.

3. Feel yourself connect with your body and its usual state. Feel your feet on the ground and your body and mind strong.

....

The Tools

Now on to the tools and techniques you will need to work with Cosmic Energy. Later in the book we will develop these in greater depth, but for now the techniques in this chapter will give you a good grounding and demonstrate Cosmic Energy in action. So read on to learn about the tools that help you harness the power of Cosmic Energy.

Visualisation

As we have seen with the work of Masaru Emoto and Professor Wiseman, thoughts are things and can really impact on your life. We've all heard of the phrase 'the power of positive thinking'. Well, now I'm going to show you how to take this one step further using the tool of visualisation.

In essence, visualisation is simply mental imagery. I often meet people who believe they cannot visualise. For example, they may attend a meditation group but as the teacher tells them to imagine they are walking down a leafy lane, they simply can't create this image in their minds. Or, I usually find that they do indeed build the image but they cannot believe in it, because their expectation is that the experience will be the same as actually standing in the leafy lane. I always ask these people, 'What colour is your front door?' As they reply 'red' or 'white', I explain to them that the only way they can access this information is by recalling an image that they had previously built! If you recall the colour of your front door, you are using a stored mental image to construct your visualisation.

I want you to know that you can visualise; and an important point to emphasise here is that you can only ever achieve what you can visualise – so if you want to be a millionaire but cannot imagine yourself living in a big house with a pool, it will never happen. This tool is an important part of connecting with Cosmic Energy because it uses the power of your mind; it creates a link between your hopes and dreams and the universe. In short, visualisation is the bridge that carries your message to the universe.

....

Building the Picture

This simple exercise will help you to build your visualising skills. Always take time to work on one single image. It may be of the room you are in right now.

1. Carry out the opening up technique on page 23.

2. Look around the room then close your eyes and recreate in your mind the image you have just seen.

   ◆ What colour are the curtains? Is the furniture soft or hard?

   ◆ Now bring in your other senses. What does the room smell like?

   ◆ Are there any sounds, maybe a fridge buzzing, a bird chirping outside, a plane overhead?

   ◆ What does the room feel like? Is it hot or cold?

By using all your senses you will find you can visualise more strongly.

3. Now focus on the image and make it more clearly defined. Keep coming back to the one image, and each time make it clearer and clearer.

4. Carry out the closing down technique on page 24.

Each time you build the image and use your senses you increase the strength of the energy, making it more powerful, more focused and more likely to happen. As your visualising skills grow, so will your ability to manifest.

....

Manifesting

Manifesting is a method you can use to make things happen, to realise your dreams and to influence the outcome of events. To manifest, you connect with Cosmic Energy in its purest form. Today, we are becoming increasingly aware of our ability to manifest. It is not uncommon to hear people utter something negative then say, 'Oops – if I don't watch out, that will happen!' Our thoughts contain Cosmic Energy, so what we focus on becomes our reality. So if we focus on problems these are what we attract, but if we focus on our dreams and desires in a clear way they become reality – and occur often within a very short space of time.

Top Tip

If you catch yourself thinking something negative, just say, 'Negate that thought. I am positive.' This will cancel out the negative energy. With practice, your negative thoughts will occur less and less.

The mind is our control centre; it is our receiver of information and our transmitter. We know that we can hear, see and talk, but we can also send out and receive messages over far distances simply using the power of our thoughts. We can influence events and others and draw to us what we want.

Telepathy

This is the ability to send a thought, or information, from one person to another using only the power of the mind. Telepathy can occur with someone in the same room or with another person thousands of miles away.

I like to think of telepathy as thought vibrations like telephone cables linking into the hub of the universe and then going out again to the person you want to contact. I know that if I send feelings to someone they are more than likely to get through – that they will sense my energy towards them – and I find that my friends can pick up information about me, too. Last year my friend Leslie called and asked me if I was okay. She'd been sitting watching television when she clearly heard me call her name. We live some sixty miles apart and have been close friends since childhood. At that time my mother was very ill and had just been rushed into hospital.

I can focus on another old friend of mine, Bobby, and make him telephone me. At times this exasperates him because he cannot get me out of his head until he calls; he's even rung me with the opening line, 'What do you want – I am busy!'

Almost everyone has had an incident of thinking about someone only for them to phone soon afterwards. Or you may have thought of a song from long ago only for it to come on the radio or someone starts to hum the same tune. Telepathy happens so often that we almost take it for granted, yet are delighted when it occurs. Wouldn't it be amazing if you could use telepathy at will instead of it being a random incident that occurs once in a blue moon? For some of you it may happen daily, weekly, or monthly – but I bet it's still not under your control. Later in this book I will teach you some tried-and-tested techniques that will enable you to send someone a telepathic message. I will also show you how to use telepathy to attract someone's attention when you need to and even send thoughts, sensations, images and ideas to a person of your choice. Imagine how useful it will be to influence someone who is being stubborn over an idea. With telepathy, you can get your point across first before anyone has had a chance to disagree. Whether it's regarding love, work or any other situation, popping an opinion an into someone's head can make a huge difference to a dilemma.

Telepathy or mind transference is a wonderful skill to develop,

and, as I've explained earlier in this chapter, it's a natural part of
our primal self; we seem to accept radio waves floating across
space, and the way in which telepathy works is not so different.
Thought waves can travel any distance at any time.

Sigmund Freud was a sceptic regarding psychic matters, but
even he believed telepathy to be 'a regressive, primitive faculty
that was lost in the course of evolution, but which still has the
ability to manifest itself under certain conditions'. Many scep-
tics allow the possibility of telepathy because they have
experienced it first hand. Most stories about telepathy relate to
extreme events when senses are heightened, such as times of
great distress, like war – telepathy is our primal self coming to
the surface to look after us. Many stories collected involve
knowing when someone close is in trouble or in pain, and have
been contacted or saved by a loved one picking up the telepathic
message.

There is a huge amount of evidence for telepathy, and if I
wrote down all the studies I have come across it would fill a
book of its own. Notably, in the 1960s the Maimonides Medical
Center in Brooklyn carried out numerous studies into the
subject. Later, the data was analysed at the University of
California, which discovered that the telepathic information
related in the case studies had an accuracy rate of 84 per cent.
More recently, twins researcher Guy Playfair came to the
conclusion that 30 per cent of twins experience telepathy. In a
1997 television programme he took four pairs of identical
twins and wired up one of each pair to monitor their brain
waves, blood pressure and galvanic skin response. He put the
other twins in a soundproofed room some distance away. The
four twins who were not wired up were suddenly shocked by a
loud alarm on the back of their chairs, yet their twins who were

being monitored reacted as if they had been shocked– although they had not actually heard the noise. When questioned, the wired-up twins had no idea what had happened, but something inside them registered the unexpected noise.

In later chapters I will show you some simple but very effective methods of using telepathy and give you the real key to making sure the message gets through loud and clear.

Meditation

Meditation is a key tool that connects you directly to the universal force – Cosmic Energy – by taking you into an altered state of awareness. There are many methods of meditation, but most involve relaxing, calming your mind and focusing on your breathing.

One of the great things about meditation is that it allows you to put your everyday life to one side. It clears your mind and creates a connection between your earthly self and the universe. By relaxing deeply and clearing your mind you will find meditation more powerful than simply visualising.

Meditation is central to Buddhism. The Buddha gained enlightenment while in a deep meditation. There are early records of meditation all over the world. Some of the oldest records are from India, where it is a natural part of the everyday Hindu life. But meditation is also found in all major religions, including Christianity, Islam and Judaism.

Meditation gives us a clear pathway to connect with Cosmic Energy. It allows us to be unencumbered by the debris of our daily thoughts, events and feelings.

Many of the exercises in this book use meditation techniques to access Cosmic Energy.

Working with the Aura

The aura is quite simply the human energy field. Years ago people would laugh if you said you had an aura, but now there is enough scientific evidence to prove we all have one. In my first book *Instant Intuition* I gave many examples of the scientific work in this field and how, as far back as 1800, the German physician and astrologer Franz Anton Mesmer believed the human body had an aura, and that this energy could affect another person. It seems our ancient selves were aware of auras too – if you look at paintings of Buddha, Christ and other spiritual leaders they invariably are depicted with a halo – an aura so bright people could see it.

We tend to be aware of our solid selves, our physical body, and less aware of our more subtle energy fields. To become aware of your aura you simply need to imagine it around you. Start to notice when you are in a queue and you can 'feel' someone standing too close. Or when you are feeling happy your energy field will expand and somehow you will feel 'brighter'. There may be times when you want to reach out to someone but for various reasons cannot, but you may notice that you will send them a little of your energy. Your aura will reach out to them and, as it does, you will feel a connection with that person.

Turning up Your Aura

The first time you try this technique you will need to find a quiet place and relax. After a few practice runs, you will be able to do this anywhere and at any time.

1. Begin with the opening up technique (see page 23)

2. Close your eyes and imagine your aura surrounding you. Just visualise feeling your aura and don't worry too much about actually seeing it. Simply build a picture in your mind's eye of it stretching out from your body.

3. Now see that the colours are made up of energy, which dances around you. Take your first impressions to find out your colours. Try it now. Immediately think of the first three colours that come into your mind. They may appear visually as colours, or as words, or you may 'hear' them. In whatever way you pick up this information, your instant intuition has just told you three of the colours in your aura.

4. Once you know the colours of your aura you can begin to visualise them around you. A great exercise is to sit quietly and imagine your aura. Be aware of how each colour feels. Next, imagine increasing the brightness of each colour to make your aura really shine and glisten. As the colours increase in intensity you will feel the characteristics of that colour flow through you. It feels marvellous.

5. Now experience the energy vibrating and shining and be aware that this energy is part of you and so it can be controlled by you.

6. Finish with the closing down technique (see page 24).

....

Later in the book you can learn about the colours of your aura and how to work with them (see pages 158, 171).

The Etheric Energy Technique (EET)

As you become aware of your own aura and its vibration, you will become conscious of a subtler part – Etheric Energy. If you have ever had your aura photographed you will immediately have been struck by its bright colours; but if you look closer you will see a more subtle energy surrounding it. This subtle energy usually shows up as a grey or silvery shimmer – this is your Etheric Energy and the part of your aura you can manipulate and use in various techniques. In *Instant Intuition,* I introduced Etheric Energy Techniques and showed the reader how to use EET to tap into people no matter where they were in the world and find out what they were thinking or feeling. In fact, it can be used to benefit many areas of your life, but your first step if you have never worked with it before is to become aware of your own Etheric Energy.

Getting to Know Your Etheric Energy

This is a process I taught in *Instant Intuition*. It is important to master this because we will be using it in later exercises.

1. Carry out the opening up technique on page 23.

2. Become aware of your aura and feel its energy. Imagine making it brighter or duller. Now imagine the glow of the Etheric Energy surrounding your aura. Once you have an awareness of your Etheric Energy you can do amazing things with it.

3. Imagine moving the Etheric Energy, stretching it. Hold out your arms in front of you and imagine the Etheric Energy stretching way beyond them, extending two, three and four metres out in front of you. Now, bring the energy back to your body.

4. Next, allow your Etheric Energy to make a pointed shape on the top of your head like a dunce's hat. Then bring it back. Play around and try out some ideas of your own.

5. This is the important part. Now that you have 'found' your Etheric Energy, focus on your solar plexus area and imagine your Etheric Energy forming a shape a little like an arm and allow this to stretch out in front of you.

6. Now think of someone that you come across in your every-day life. Maybe a colleague or friend, ideally someone that you would find it useful to know what they are feeling. Now take your Etheric Energy 'arm' and gently place the 'hand' on their solar plexus. This area is the seat of all emotion and this is where you will find out exactly what you need to know. Take your immediate impression. Do not censor it.

7. When you are finished, bring your Etheric Energy arm back into your body and surround yourself with bright white light for a few moments.

8. Carry out the closing down technique on page 24 to finish the session.

Take time to get to know your Etheric Energy because we will be using it a great deal throughout this book. It's a wonderful energy tool, it can be used to protect you, find out what others think and send messages for you – once you learn to utilise its power it will be a powerful ally.

Thought Field Therapy

Thought Field Therapy (TFT) involves tapping with the fingers at meridian points on the upper body and hands to heal a variety of mental and physical ailments. It works along the same lines as acupuncture – but without the needles, obviously!

I first came across TFT during a healing session in which the therapist tapped on the side of my head several times and my headache vanished immediately. He then tapped on my hand and reduced my craving for tea. I was intrigued, to say the least.

Two days later there was a feature in a newspaper about Thought Field Therapy helping people to stop smoking. Later that day a chap named Gerard came to see me. He told me that he had trained in Thought Field Therapy under Dr Roger Callahan, who developed the therapy, and how he used it to clear anything from trauma to phobias and addictions. I have long since learnt to take notice if something pops up repeatedly in a short space of time, so I decided to investigate by reading Dr Callahan's book, *Tapping the Healer Within*. Roger Callahan discovered TFT almost by chance. Dr Callahan was a 'by the book' psychologist, with a PhD in clinical psychology from Syracuse University and holding the post of Associate Professor and Director of Psychological Services and Research at

Michigan University. Roger had always been open to new approaches and, like many of his colleagues, was disappointed by the lack of success of the traditional talking-based therapies. He saw many people with phobias, depression or relationship issues who talked endlessly about their problems often for months, or even years, yet with traditional therapy they were simply not getting any better. Roger commented how he and a number of his fellow psychologists often discussed their dismal track records, with few clients recovering. But then came a huge turning point, via a patient named Mary.

Mary had the most intense water phobia Roger had ever come across. The sight of water almost paralysed her – she could not bath her children, was terrified of rain and had terrifying night-mares that the ocean was 'getting her'.

Roger tried every therapy he had available but nothing worked. On one occasion he managed to actually get her to sit by his pool, but the poor woman was desperately upset and described sitting there as 'sheer torture'. In that moment Roger had a flash of inspiration. He knew a little about Chinese medi-cine and how energy flows along meridian lines that correspond with acupuncture points. Mary had said that she felt a sickening feeling in the pit of her stomach, so he instructed her to tap on the energy point just under her eye because it corresponds with the stomach meridian. Within minutes Mary lit up and said, 'It's gone, the awful feeling in my stomach has gone.' She ran down to his pool, dipped her feet in and splashed water on her face. Roger thought she had gone mad. Later that day, she faced the ultimate test. She drove to the ocean during a storm and waded waist deep into the rushing waves. To this day, over twenty years later, the sickening feeling has never returned.

Roger Callahan then began to experiment with tapping and by trial and error he found that certain sequences or algorithms work with certain problems. Today the success rate can be as high as 98 per cent, unheard of in any other therapy.

Thought Field Therapy and Trauma Patients

Thought Field Therapy is now an established form of treatment with open-minded therapists working in the complementary medicine field. In fact, TFT was used on the most difficult cases in Kosovo in 2000 when 105 victims of ethnic violence received TFT from an international volunteer group of therapists. These people were suffering from post-traumatic stress as a result of rape and torture; some had seen their loved ones massacred. The chief medical officer in Kosovo, Dr Shkelzen Syla, sent a letter of appreciation to the group of volunteers, headed up by Professor Carl Johnson, who sits on the American Board of Professional Psychology. It read: 'Many well-funded relief organisations have treated the post-traumatic stress here in Kosovo. Some of our people had limited improvement, but Kosovo had no major change or real hope until volunteer American Professor Carl Johnson came to help us . . . with Thought Field Therapy. We referred our most difficult trauma patients to the Professor. The success rate from TFT was 100 per cent for every patient.'

In later chapters I am going to teach you how to use TFT to clear the effects of your own trauma and overcome fears (see pages 90–2).

Crystals and Gemstones

Crystals and gemstones carry their own unique vibrations. Our bodies are greatly influenced by them and their frequency can change our own frequency, and so by having the right crystals, or gemstones, on your person you can clear negative energies, attract good vibrations and improve your ability to manifest.

Each semi-precious stone has a gift for you. My spiritual teacher Greta had a full selection in her healing space and her home. At the beginning of each day she would focus on them and decide which she needed for that particular day. She would then meditate holding her stone to receive its message and energy, then carry it with her throughout that day. I began to do the same and found that I became more in harmony with the day's events.

Buying Crystals

When buying your own crystals and gemstones, take your time. The seller will understand that you need to focus and not be rushed. Once a stone has attracted your attention, pick it up and hold it in your dominant hand and notice how it feels. You may notice a tingling or vibration. The stone may become hotter or colder. You may suddenly feel quite different – happier or calmer. Thoughts may pop into your head. Accept whatever happens as the stone's personal message to you.

Many people believe that you do not choose a crystal but in fact the crystal chooses you. You may find a crystal and if so, the crystal has found you. Or you might be browsing in a shop and one crystal will seem to be calling you – something will make it stand out. That is your crystal. It is as if one will be calling, 'Over here, over here!'

Crystals also know when their work with you is done and will simply disappear. Many people have told me things like, 'It was on my desk for years then suddenly one day it was gone. I turned the place over looking for it' or, 'A hole appeared in my new handbag just where I keep my crystal. And even though it was in my car, I never found it.'

The Key Crystals and Gemstones and Their Benefits

◆ Agate: Good for mental stability and awakens latent talents.

◆ Amber: One of my favourites for clients suffering love pain. It soaks up the negative energy, rebalances, then gives strength, all in the blink of an eye.

◆ Amethyst: Good for calming, also promotes spirituality and on a business side gives flexibility in decision-making.

◆ Bloodstone: Perfect for detoxing – and to create balance if you overindulge in food and alcohol.

◆ Citrine: Good if you cannot stop crying. This is the stone to give to a friend who is devastated by problems caused by love, work, family – everything and anything.

◆ Emerald: This is said to be the jewel of love and truth. I use this for clients who have had their heart broken and find it hard to trust again.

◆ Fluorite: An all-round health booster, helps fight against common viral infections like colds, flu and cold sores.

◆ Garnet: The one to pick if you want a confidence boost and to allow sexual confidence to flow. On a business level, promotes determination and direction.

- Hematite: Helps you to radiate a soft loving energy, health-wise good for fighting against insomnia.

- Moonstone: Clears patterns of attracting partners who cheat. Also known as the traveller's stone because it protects against the perils of travel.

- Obsidian: If you are feeling negative, this is the stone for you. It can evaporate thoughts of hatred towards those of love.

- Rose quartz: This stone sends out a big message to the universe: 'I am ready for love!' This is also good for clearing the skin and reducing pain.

- Ruby: A love booster, it aids fertility and enhances passion.

- Smoky quartz: Promotes co-operation and practicality in money matters.

- Tektite: Clears up bad energies. Wonderful if you have been involved with someone who turned out to be very badly behaved. Also clears feelings of anger.

- Tiger's eye: Promotes independence, helping people who are too needy. Also eases congestion of the bowels, throat and eyes.

- Tourmaline: Gives confidence when you feel weak and need a little 'backbone'.

- Turquoise: Heals childhood trauma and stops you from repeating patterns.

Using Your Crystals and Gems

1. Wash your crystal or gem under running water then soak it for at least one hour in spring water with added sea salt. Allow it to dry naturally. You can leave it on a windowsill at night to charge it with either moon energy or in daylight for solar energy. However, do not leave a crystal ball in direct sunlight as it can project extreme heat, which can be dangerous.

2. Now hold your stone in both hands and allow yourself to relax. Clear your mind of all thoughts and feel your crystal or gem energy blend with your own energy. Feel it become part of you. Feel the stone's energy flowing to you and your energy flowing towards the stone. Feel the energies blend.

3. Breathe into your hands and into the crystal or gem. Every out-breath will flow into the crystal or gem giving it your own energy and creating a powerful link. You begin life with your first breath and end life with your last breath. Your breath is the essence of you that exists in the here-and-now. By breathing this energy into your stone, you build the most powerful connection and gain incredible benefits. Spend time relaxing and breathing as you hold your stone.

As you send your breath to your crystal or gem you breathe life into it. You awaken its potent force and enable it to do its work.

Aroma

The power of smell has been used by the Chinese, Romans and Native Americans, and in India, the Middle East, Mesopotamia, Egypt and Greece. In ancient times, rare perfumes were highly prized and cost vast amounts of money. Aromas are mentioned in all religious texts to be used to produce altered states or to connect with a higher energy. The gifts from the three wise men when Jesus were born besides gold were frankincense and myrrh.

Even in today's modern society we are aware of the effects of smell. Think back to when you experienced the smell of the sea, or fresh-cut grass or a forest. Aroma triggers memories and emotions – think of fresh strawberries, coffee, freshly baked bread or your grandmother's cooking.

I remember once walking in London when I smelt 'Afghanistan'. It's a very distinct smell with a rich combination of food, incense dust and animals. I was immediately transported back to one of my favourite places and gained a great sense of happiness and warmth. It is important to work with your own associations and to use the aromas (usually in the form of essential oils) that are pleasing to you.

Key Aromas and Their Benefits

Please take care when using essential oils if you are pregnant, as some of them can be dangerous during pregnancy. And when using oil burners, please remember that the water does evaporate so you need to keep an eye on the water level. As with all candles, make sure you are safe. Remember, never ever leave a burning candle unattended.

- Cardamom: Puts a spring in your step and aids youthfulness.

- Frankincense: Cleopatra loved it and it has been used by the Catholic Church during mass for centuries. It is very spiritual and will cleanse your environment and protect you. If you are having relationship problems, it can help 'clear the air'.

- Grapefruit: Gives confidence and energy and lifts your spirits so it's ideal before a party. I have seen clients beam with happiness after a bout of depression just with this one smell.

- Jasmine: Many years ago in North Africa I caught an unusual smell. I asked a local man what it was and he told me 'jasmine'. He picked me a flower from his garden and told me to wear it in my hair, and added, 'You will always have love in your life if you have jasmine with you. This is why our women always smile.' It's a wonderful scent if you feel lost and alone. It sends a message out to the universe that you have love in your heart that you want to share with someone special.

- Lavender: Who hasn't smelt lavender on a summer's day and immediately felt peaceful? We have some growing near my office and as soon as I smell it, I smile. It is known to help you relax, aid restful sleep and relieve tension headaches.

- Lemon: Cleanses after illness, hurt, or if someone leaves a bad atmosphere.

- Mandarin: I call this the smiley smell. It is almost childlike especially when you have been feeling negative or hopeless as in – 'I won't ever meet anyone.'

◆ Nutmeg: This can also be used in a warm drink. It is soothing and comforting. If you are feeling vulnerable, drinking nutmeg in frothy milk is like being wrapped in a warm blanket.

◆ Orange blossom: Fantastic for helping anxiety, shock, panic and heart palpitations.

◆ Peppermint: The Romans loved peppermint. When too much has been going on peppermint will clear the way and calm things down. It's also a good for the digestion.

◆ Rose: Very good to use after trauma, grief, or great sadness. Helps the emotions to heal.

◆ Rosemary: A wonderful stimulant especially if you are lacking energy or get-up-and-go in your work or personal life. A client recently told me she needs to go out and meet someone, but after a hard day's work and long commute home she flops into the chair and cannot muster the energy. A spray of rosemary and she took up dancing and met the love of her life. When he told her he was attracted to her vibrancy, she laughed and said, 'He wouldn't have said that if he'd seen me a short time ago before I started using my rose-mary spray.'

◆ Sandalwood: From India and used for over 4,000 years, mentally soothing and relaxing.

◆ Ylang ylang: Good for people who work too hard and find they are getting overly sensitive or irritable, and quarrel-some in their relationships. Instead of an annoyance causing an argument, you shrug your shoulders and think, 'So what?'

Bach Flower Remedies

Bach Flower Remedies were developed by Dr Edward Bach, a successful Harley Street physician, bacteriologist and homeopath. He had a strong belief that much illness comes from the personality and gave up his lucrative doctor's practice to develop his remedies.

During his research he discovered what he classed as '38 negative states' and the corresponding plants to cure them – there are remedies for everything from anxiety, to impatience to lack of confidence. The premise for his treatment is that a flower remedy can change a negative vibration into a positive vibration.

Throughout this book I will be showing you how to use Bach Flower Remedies to help clear any negative vibrations that have been holding you back or blocking your path to wellbeing and achieving your full potential.

Here is a small selection of some of the Bach Flower Remedies and the conditions they can be used to treat.

Key Bach Flower Remedies and Their Benefits

♦ Agrimony: Suitable for people who put a brave face on their problems or mask sadness with addictions. Creates a true inner happiness.

♦ Centaury: Good for weak-willed people who are bossed around and cannot say no. Creates a strong inner strength.

♦ Cerato: Can be helpful for over-talkative individuals who drain the energy of others by attention-seeking. Gives quiet confidence.

◆ Chicory: Creates awareness of others and a more giving nature. Ideal to help possessive, selfish types who feel the world owes them a living change their way of thinking.

◆ Clematis: Beneficial for sleepy daydreamers to become fully present and excited by all areas of their lives.

◆ Gentian: Promotes a feeling of focus, good for negative individuals who become discouraged by setbacks. It can help them keep going no matter how large the obstacle.

◆ Impatiens: Perfect for jumpy, impatient types who are never off duty as this creates a relaxed attitude to life and the influences around them.

◆ Mimulus: Overcomes shyness and fear of known things such as public speaking, flying and spiders. Creates the courage to face fears and enjoy life.

◆ Rock Rose: Brings great courage; good for when someone is terrified or in a state of panic.

◆ Scleranthus: Balances out mood swings, and the emotions of being unreliable and indecisive. Brings calm and balance.

◆ Vervain: Good for anyone who is tense, highly strung and sensitive. Creates a quiet strength in the face of difficulties.

◆ Water violet: Creates a more flexible approach to people with rigid opinions and outlook, also softens attitudes and promotes a more sympathetic view of others.

Colour

From the moment you open your eyes in the morning you are influenced by colour. From your home décor, food and clothes to the colour of your car or lipstick, colour is everywhere and can change your energy and the way you feel in an instant.

Our world is a kaleidoscope of colour from a beautiful sunset and autumn leaves to the rosy cheeks on a new-born baby. We cringe at colours that clash and our mouths water at the sight of beautifully coloured food, yet certain colours actually turn people off eating and are never used by food companies, such as blue and purple.

Notice how the colours we wear reflect the time we are living in. People turn to grey and black in a recession. Have you noticed too that when there is a downturn in the economy, there is a resurgence of Gothic style? By constrast, in boom times such as the 1980s, people tend to wear bright colours; watch quiz shows from this period and you will be surprised by how bright the men's shirts and ladies clothes are in the programmes.

Have you ever moved into a new home where you hated the colours? A quick lick of paint and hey presto – your home feels so much better. In my early twenties I moved into a house where the front room had been painted black and bright red. Every visitor would yawn within minutes of arriving and no one stayed for long. I soon changed to neutral relaxing colours with the odd splash of light and dark blue. The transformation was dramatic, as was the room's energy, and my visitors soon felt vibrant and happy there.

None of this knowledge is new; the power of colour has featured in all ancient civilisations. For example, Egyptian temples contained special healing rooms that were constructed to allow the dissipation of the rays of the sun into the colours of the rainbow.

Throughout this book you will find many colour suggestions.

Colour is a doorway, a starting point which leads deep into the mind and soul. It has the ability to affect all living things both consciously and unconsciously.

Theo Gimbel

Sound

Sound is one of the most powerful ways to create and change energy. The vibration of sound affects us on so many levels, yet it is unseen. You can change how you feel within seconds simply by playing music; there is music to calm you down or move you to tears. By listening to a particular song or classical piece you can change how you feel – from being worn-out to bursting with energy and wanting to dance around your living room. You can become lost in music and it can take you into an altered state – yet it can also force you to turn down the radio because a tune has come on that annoys you. Many times I have left shops because the canned music has agitated me so much. If you have any doubt that sound produces great effect, just think of how a glass can shatter to a high-pitched note or how the sound of a dripping tap has been used as an instrument of torture.

The use of sound is as old as time. From mantras to chants, songs to battle roars, it is part of our natural primal self.

The sound of your voice carries far more influence than you can ever imagine. Former Prime Minister Margaret Thatcher lowered her voice tone in order to be taken more seriously. Stop for a moment and think about someone who has a grating or screeching voice. You are very liable to actually have a physical response as you cringe at the thought. Now think of someone with a beautiful voice and immediately you feel your shoulders relax and you begin to smile.

The following exercise will help you get to grips with the power of your own voice vibration.

Voice Vibration

◆ Choose a sentence, for instance, 'I hope the sun is shining tomorrow.'

◆ Say this sentence in an aggressive tone, now in a soft and gentle voice, now using a sultry and sexy approach. Finally, say the sentence in an exasperated tone. You will feel a subtle difference as you say the sentence in different tones.

◆ Repeat the exercise once more but say it with a huge grin on your face. How did that feel and sound?

You have just created energy through sound, and you created energy by putting emotion into the sound. By combining emotion with sound you can produce something that wasn't there before, an energy that can stir feelings and emotions in yourself and in others. How powerful is that?

You can create a mood, and change how other people feel just by the tone of your voice or the music you play. Many experienced party hosts know to slow down the music when they think it is time people started to leave. Supermarkets play music that puts people into a slight trance so that they spend more money by shopping unconsciously, and fast-food restaurants have upbeat music so that you eat and leave quickly making way for the next customer and more money in their tills. Several English towns have even taken to playing laid-back music such as Des O'Connor over loud speakers in town centre trouble spots because it brings down the vandalism rate.

As well as being a mood-changer, sound is wonderful for clearing negative energy from your body, mind and home. Sound can heal and it can help us fall in love, and it can connect us to the universal energy. Yet we rarely stop to hear. We so often are surrounded by noise yet do not notice the beauty of sound. Stop in silence, listen and become aware of different sounds and how they affect you.

Sound is alive, it floats through solid walls, it floats out into space and into the universe and beyond, it vibrates through our bodies.

Throughout this book we will be discovering and working with the power of sound, using it to change how you feel and to create energy. You will even learn how the sound of your name carries an energy. We will look at how you can use sound to create a greater harmony with yourself and connect to the universal energy.

Sound seems to be the simplest, easiest and most powerful tool for transformation I have come across.

Jonathan Goldman

Astral Travel

The body is split into two parts: the physical body, which is the part you can see, and feel, and the astral body, which is your spiritual being. Astral travel (often called an out-of-the-body experience (OBE)) occurs when your astral body journeys to other realms. Some people can astral-travel at will.

In effect, an OBE is just your own essence, your own Etheric Energy, leaving the body. It feels natural and it feels wonderful. Many people experience astral travel during sleep. They dream they are flying, floating or even falling. I have met many people who have told me stories of how they dreamt they were somewhere new, only at a later date to discover the exact place. Or they have visited someone during an OBE and seen what they were doing, only to later discover they were correct regarding specific details.

You may have heard stories of people leaving their body for a few moments when they have had a near-death experience during an accident, operation or heart attack. During the shock they have been forced out of their body very suddenly. Later they describe seeing and hearing things they could not have seen or heard.

Carl, a client of mine, told me, 'I was very ill in hospital with pneumonia. At times I dreamt or thought I was dreaming that I was at home with my wife and children. I actually heard them talking about taking me on holiday to Florida when I got better. I heard my wife say that a colleague of hers had recently bought a villa to let out and she could get it at a good price. When I got better and told her, she was astounded. We are logical people and couldn't get our heads around the fact that somehow I was there with them while my body was in a coma in hospital.'

Many doctors have admitted their patients have told them of

events that have happened in other parts of the hospital that they simply could not have known about while they were desperately ill or even momentarily dead. Everyone who has told me about their experiences has said the experience was not vague but graphic and in great detail.

One of the first pioneers in this field was Robert Monroe, a radio broadcaster, who began to undergo out-of-body experiences several times a week spontaneously and without willing it. When he began his research in 1958, little was known about such things. He said, 'It was not during sleep, so I couldn't dismiss it as a simple dream. I had full, conscious awareness of what was happening, which of course only made it worse. I assumed it was some sort of a hallucination caused by something dangerous – a brain tumour, or impending mental illness. Or imminent death.'

Monroe fought to get back into his body time and time again but could never stop it from happening. After seeking medical help, his doctor told him that various ancient societies, including Indian yogis, had beliefs about leaving their bodies. He amassed a wealth of information and began studying, exploring to find out everything he possibly could about this subject. Monroe began taking control of his travels. In time, he met other travellers on the astral plane. His ground-breaking book about his experiences is entitled *Journeys out of the Body*.

Monroe came to the conclusion that we are 'a vibrational pattern comprised of many interacting and resonating frequencies'. Today, the Monroe Institute carries on his research into human consciousness. Dr Sam Parnia has also carried out ground-breaking studies in this field and recounts some amazing stories in his book *What Happens When We Die?*

You may be interested to know that a study by Erika

Bouguignon looked at 488 world societies and found that 437 had a belief in OBEs, from Hindus to Native Americans; and these cultures' experiences of OBEs are rife and incredibly similar.

But how does this connect to Cosmic Energy? It's simple – the astral level is like a giant mirror reflecting reality back to us. Everything we do on a physical level affects the astral, and everything we do on the astral affects the physical. The thoughts you think travel out to the astral, which is how we manifest. Be careful what you think, say and do, and be careful what you ask for because you will get it thanks to the power of Cosmic Energy. Later in this book I am going to teach you how to manifest from the astral level, and how to communicate with others – especially with those who are hard to talk to. You will also discover how to improve your health, lose weight and discover your true purpose using astral travel.

Top Tip

Using multiple tools creates a more powerful and synergistic effect. For example, using colour, sound and aroma (in the form of essential oils) together creates a layer effect of energy. By adding powerful visualisations, the results at times can be astonishing.

Throughout the book, I will show you how to use the tools in this chapter individually, and also how to use them in groups. You can enjoy trying and experimenting with the different effects the tools produce.

You now have a good grounding of the most powerful tools I will be exploring and working with in this book. You are about to discover how to use Cosmic Energy to attract love and strengthen existing relationships.

CHAPTER 3
Love is All Around You

You were born open to love. As a tiny baby you gave and received love unconditionally, your love energy flowing with nothing to block its path. You never thought, 'I'd better hold back here because this person may not like the look of me or they may hurt me.' You never worried that things could go wrong or that you might make a fool of yourself.

But as you grew, you were given blocks. You saw relationships break up, someone you expected to love you didn't love you back; you saw people behave badly and you saw others heart-broken. At some point these experiences also caused you to feel rejected, hurt, snubbed or foolish. A tiny dot of wariness grew and grew, which stopped you from claiming the unconditional love you deserve.

People are often brought up to have a negative view of marriage and long-term relationships. They are influenced by their family history and seeing people close to them go through the worst times during a break-up, along with the onslaught of negative television programmes and films that focus on infidelity and the theme that you 'can't trust anybody but yourself'.

In this chapter I am going to show you how you can break out of this negative way of thinking, which will be your first major step in helping you to manifest love. If you are in a relationship, I will show you how to make it more trusting and fulfilling. I'm also going to be looking at the following areas:

1. Are you ready for love?

2. How to manifest your dream partner

3. How to spot 'the one'

4. How to build a happy relationship

5. Overcome conflict with a lover

6. Rekindle a romance from the past

7. How to break free from a past love

You are about to discover how to overcome the blocks to love energy. Often, blocks can be so ingrained in us we are unaware we have them – if we were aware, we would change our patterns immediately. So take time over this next section and note anything specific that rings a bell or any patterns that seem somehow familiar.

Are You Ready For Love?

Have you noticed how some people seem to attract suitors like moths around a flame while others remain stubbornly single? I have been studying and observing love energy for over 30 years. Time and time gain I observe the same patterns. I notice that some people are surrounded by love while others are lonely. I also noticed that some of the most beautiful-looking people were also the loneliest – good love energy seemed to have nothing to do with looks, money, prestige or personality. It also had no connection with how much or how little effort they put in, or how good they were at the game of life or as a person.

Richard Bandler, co-developer of Neuro-Linguistic Programming (NLP), says, 'We seem to study people who have had a problem finding the answer when in fact we should be studying those who have got it right.' So I began to watch people who were successful in love and I came to the conclusion that these people have aligned their energy with the universal energy. Somehow they were open to love. Others 'thought' they were ready and open, but by asking them just two or three questions I could tell they were not yet in the right place for the right partner to enter their lives.

Take the Love Test

For my love workshops, I devised a series of questions for participants. The answers reveal if a person really is ready for love. I would like you to read each question yourself and then answer it spontaneously – just write down the first response that comes into your mind. In accepting this immediate re-action, you are tapping into your love energy and will reveal your true feelings. Be prepared to be surprised.

Remember, it is important that you answer these questions spontaneously.

1. **If your perfect partner walked into your life right this very second, how would you feel?**
   Write down your response NOW.

2. **You have just received a phone call to say that the love of your life is sitting in your home right now waiting for you. What would be your reaction?**
   Write down your response NOW.

3. The love of your life is out socialising, hoping to meet you. What do you think about this statement?
Write down your response NOW.

Please spend a few moments looking at your answers. What do you think they tell you about how you really feel about love? Do you see any patterns emerging? Is there an area, a theme, like your self-esteem or family, which keeps cropping up in your responses?

Here's a selection of the responses I have received in my workshops over the years to the same three questions.

1. If your perfect partner walked into your life right this very second, how would you feel?
'I'd be embarrassed, I don't have any make-up on.'
'Self-conscious. I need to lose a little weight.'
'Terrible. I have my old grey pants on. Supposing things got passionate?'
'I'm so busy with work I don't know how I would have time for them.'
Another favourite that I hear often is, 'My kids are still living at home and they play up if I get friendly with anyone.'
Other people tell me they are absolutely and completely ready.

2. You have just received a phone call to say that the love of your life is sitting in your home right now waiting for you. What would be your reaction?
'Oh no, my home is a mess.'
'I hope they don't look in the fridge and see all the rubbish I have in there.'
'My home is so boring (scruffy/dirty), it's embarrassing.'

3. **The love of your life is out socialising, hoping to meet you. What do you think about this statement?**

    'But I hardly go anywhere so I'm not going to meet them.'

    'Well, I don't have a social life so I'm doomed to be single for ever.'

    'That's rubbish, I go to the same old places all the time and never ever meet anyone new.'

You may have already met your perfect partner and are very happy together, or you have chosen to be alone for the moment. If this is your situation, then great – your energy flow is fine. However, if you are actively looking for love right now and have not yet found it there is something in the way energetically, stopping you from meeting 'the one'. The response from your higher self has just given you an indication that you are putting up blocks in all sorts of guises: emotional, physical and mental. But the good news is you can clear these blocks and align your energy, which will allow an abundance of love to come in to your life. This is what I'm going to teach you in this chapter. But for the moment, I would like you to explore further why you are on your own.

Why You Are Single

From years of helping people in this area and working with energy in all aspects of people's lives, I've discovered that the only way to be truly ready for love is to remove the blocks and raise your Cosmic Energy vibration. When your vibration is low, you keep your perfect partner out of reach. To attract your perfect love your vibration needs to be vibrant and high. Your love energy needs to be flowing. Just imagine what happens to your Cosmic Energy when you have just split up with someone, or have been rejected – you can actually feel your energy drop.

When this happens, that perfect person doesn't see you. You decide not go to the event at which you would have met them, or you attract someone else with a low vibration and as you can imagine, things do not go terribly well between you. Raise your love vibration and you will feel yourself become a magnet to people who also have a positive vibration.

On some level you know you are rejecting possible partners, so you try to raise your vibration by going in search of love. Or you try to make yourself feel better with a new exercise regime, by spending lots of money on clothes, fake tan make-up or a new car. But this just gives you an energy boost that soon fizzles, and within a short space of time you feel bad again. Your energy levels drop, and you are off again looking for more quick fixes.

If you get into this situation you are locked in a downward spiral – you have a boost but then slide back down again. This downward love pattern will also attract other needy people in the same situation (because like attracts like, it's the universal law, the Law of Attraction). This is not a good combination because you will drag one another down. If you are stuck in this pattern you may also become desperate –an emotion that is really triggered by loneliness.

Imagine the following scenarios:

◆ That you have just come out of a relationship in which the other person lied, cheated, criticised and generally treated you badly. How does that make you feel right now?

◆ Now imagine you have just had the most wonderful relationship. It finished because it had run its course but it left you feeling happy, glad to have met the person and full of confidence in your personality, your sexuality and your appearance. Stop for a moment and see how that makes you feel.

If you stop and focus on how each scenario makes you feel, you will notice how it affects your energy. You may even find that when focusing on each scenario you actually stand and breathe differently. Often when doing the first exercise people slump – they look down and they look unhappy. With the second exercise people stand straighter, they smile and their eyes light up.

As you imagine these scenarios, stop and feel what type of person would be attracted to you at these times. Sometimes when you have a low vibration you can become invisible, or at other times you may attract dysfunctional people. Create a positive flow of Cosmic Energy and you will glow – and wonderful people will appear in your life, offering love and appreciation.

What Lonely People do Wrong in Love

Loneliness is perhaps one of the few emotions left in our society that people don't talk about openly. You can be in a room full of people and feel lonely. It's not about being surrounded by friends, it's about connecting with other human beings. When you are unable to connect you feel cut off and frightened, and desperation creeps in.

Desperation is a negative energy because it pushes the love vibration of others away. It creates a barrier around the desperate person that actually causes the flow of love energy to bend around them and flow in the opposite direction. The result is that your love-energy level falls further and your vibration drops – and the more desperate you get the lower your vibration will go. In short, if you're desperate you will repel love.

Suitors can smell desperation and they will run a mile because it creates an energy of fear within them.

Luckily there are lots of ways to raise your vibration, and believe me people will feel it and be drawn to you. We have all noticed how some individuals seem to have people falling over themselves to speak to them while others get little attention. You are about to learn the secrets of their popularity.

How to Raise Your Vibrations and Remove Blocks to Attracting Love

Every thought you have sends a message out to the universe. Most of your thoughts are unconscious; you would be surprised at how many people believe they are very positive, yet when played a tape of themselves talking are shocked to hear just how many negative comments they made.

Recently an acquaintance, a young man called Richard, confided, 'I never seem to meet anyone – why am I always single?' In answer to his question, I reminded him how we had been at a party a few weeks before when a girl had told him that her friend liked him. He had smiled and looked pleased, but once he heard she was ten years younger he commented, 'Oh that's no good for me, the age gap is too big.' I have heard him put up the same barriers, or energy blocks, about someone's nationality, what they do for a living, even where they live – and he's never even met any of them! So when Richard asked me for advice I reminded him what he had done at the party, that he had dismissed someone who potentially could have been perfect for him. He replied, 'But she was too young, it would never have worked.' The message was lost on him that the perfect person could be standing ten feet away. I remember distinctly what happened at the party because I've seen it all before; Richard didn't even glance over to see what she looked like.

I see people behave this way all the time. They are adamant that they are not blocking love yet they dismiss social events as a waste of time, people as unsuitable and suggestions on how to find love irrelevant to them – before you've even finished the sentence. I usually end up telling them they are hard to help. Their attitudes come from limiting beliefs that we all have to some extent, but if you identify and get rid of them you will be on your first step to finding true love.

The following exercise highlights any limiting unconscious thought patterns you may be replaying in your life – the very thoughts that are creating your loneliness.

....

What's Your Barrier to Love?

Finish each sentence with the first thought that comes to mind – do not stop and think about it.

◆ All men/women are . . .

◆ When it comes to love I always . . .

◆ I tend to meet suitors who are . . .

◆ A good relationship is . . .

◆ When I am good to people . . .

◆ If you show your feelings you . . .

◆ When I think of love I feel . . .

◆ When two people have been together a long time they ...

◆ My parents had a ... attitude to marriage

◆ To be happy with one person for the rest of my life is a concept I think is ...

◆ If I meet my perfect partner I am afraid ...

◆ To have someone to love me for ever makes me feel ...

◆ Love is ...

Examine your answers. Do they show that you expect things to go wrong or not last? Or do your answers show mistrust? Do they reflect a feeling of unworthiness? Perhaps you have some positive answers, which is wonderful. Or, all your comments may reflect your openness to love and if this is you, then your love energy is high; later in this chapter I will show you how to raise it even higher.

....

If you had some negative comments in the 'What's Your Barrier to Love?' exercise, I want you to rewrite all your responses, consciously putting a positive spin on each sentence. Notice if any make you feel uncomfortable. This will highlight the areas you need to work on. For example, you may have thought:

◆ 'When it comes to love, I always pick the wrong person.' I would like you to write in your journal, 'When it comes to love, I used to always pick the wrong person but now I'm ready to find my love equal.'

◆ Or you may have thought: 'When two people have been together a long time they fall out of love.' I would like you to write in your journal: 'When two people have been together a long time they develop a deep mutual respect, trust and understanding for one another.'

Repeat the positive sentence for the statement that you identify as your biggest stumbling block as a daily affirmation until you can say it with total confidence. If you have more than one problem area in love, work through each statement at a time then move on to the next until you have worked your way through each issue.

You can add strength to your affirmations with particular Bach Flower Remedies that boost love energy. Flower remedies are wonderful for clearing inner blocks that stop you bringing love into your life or moving on from negative situations and repeating old patterns. Whenever you have a difficult time in love, the experience leaves a negative vibration that almost hangs in the air. It's the same if you have issues about being alone or you let people walk all over you. Flower remedies can quickly clear negative energy and treat fear and desperation – the two major blocks to love – and create a new wonderful vibration to take their place.

Bach Flower Remedies for Love

These are the Bach Flower Remedies I use to create a positive love vibration and to help people overcome the blocks that stop them having good relationships. Whatever your love problem, pick the right remedy for you from the list. The remedies are easy to use, and you can make them up as love spray (see page 67).

- Agrimony: To get rid of an 'empty' feeling, especially at night. Instead you will feel warm and content whether you have company or not. Agrimony is also helpful if you have a tendency to drink, take drugs or smoke when upset.

- Beech: If you are overly critical and fussy or look down on others, this remedy will help you see the good aspects of people.

- Cherry plum: To overcome desperation and despair and to combat a fear of losing control. I recommend this to people who feel they are at the end of their tether.

- Clematis: For those who feel they have missed their chance of love because they have an unrealistic, overly romantic view of how and whom their love should be. I have used this with clients who are convinced they will marry someone famous even though they have never met them; it supports a more realistic, grounded outlook.

- Crab apple: If you do not like yourself, it helps overcome feelings of self-loathing.

- Holly: To clear feelings of jealousy or revenge, or if you suffer from being overly suspicious.

- Honeysuckle: If you live in the past and cannot let go of your feelings this remedy nudges you to move on.

- Impatiens: Helps you to slow down; good for people who have a tendency to rush into relationships.

- Mimulus: A powerful remedy great for banishing the fear of being alone.

- Red chestnut: Helps you to be more assertive and is ideal if you allow people to walk all over you.

- Rescue Remedy: Perfect for shock. Helps with the effects of terrible news such as a partner's desertion. It's also a good all-round remedy for stress and anxiety in any situation, from first-date nerves to sitting an exam.

- Willow: Helps to overcome resentment, when feeling hard done by.

The Love Spray

Your own custom-made spray will be far more potent than anything you can buy in a shop. It will carry your energy and emotions and will be specially chosen by you, for you. By combining several key ingredients, you can create a powerful and vibrant love-booster.

What you need:

- A spray bottle

- Pure spring water

- A few drops of your chosen Bach Flower Remedies

- If you prefer, add a crystal from the list in Chapter 2 (see page 39)

1. Rinse the bottle thoroughly then add your spring water. If you are adding a crystal, place it into the spray bottle and leave for at least one hour. Then add a few drops of your chosen Bach Flower Remedy or Remedies. Give the ingredients a gentle shake before putting on the bottle top.

2. Now hold the bottle in your hand and think about what you want the effect of your remedies to be. For example,

perhaps you want to feel free of a destructive relationship. If so, imagine the person concerned shrinking and fading away then imagine yourself happy doing all your favourite things, with plenty of space around you. If you want love to come your way, imagine you have your perfect partner by your side. If you want a current relationship to improve, imagine how you want it to be.

3. Now breathe into the bottle, with each out-breath your life force energy will flow into the bottle. Make sure you feel the emotions you would feel if you got exactly what you want. Once you have breathed into the bottle several times and visualised the outcome you want, put the top onto the bottle and spray your room. The effect will be almost instant. Each day breathe into your vibration spray.

Top Tip

If you have a friend who always seems to be lucky in love or is in a happy long-term relationship you could ask them to visualise their happiest moments and breathe into the bottle. Their positive vibes will enhance your spray.

Once you have worked on dissolving your energy blocks, you will be ready to meet your dream partner.

How to Manifest Your Dream Partner

Over the years I have become known in many circles. Clients come to see me, they then tell their sister or best friend or brother about me, who then come along for a consultation.

After a while, I know their whole social circle and often end up really good friends with everyone. I go to their parties, weddings, lunches, PR launches and other functions.

One such circle would meet for lunch once a month. I could never understand why year in year out none of these ladies – seven in all – ever had a good relationship. On rare occasions one of them may go on a date but nothing would come of it. I would do each of them readings regularly but I never saw anything concrete in the love stakes. Yet they were lovely, fun, clever, good-looking girls. Why were they not being snapped up?

One day over lunch one of the girls, named Viv, made a comment about their man list and the others laughed. Now I have met people who swear by having a wish list, so I was curious to know about their 'must-have' criteria. I had found that if people were very clear about what they wanted they seemed to get it. So what was happening here? I pondered on this for some time and focused on getting an answer the next time the girls met.

As usual when I needed to know something the universe stepped in and brought me into contact with a lady called Pip, whom I met at a New Year's Eve party. We were chatting and when I told her I was a professional psychic she started talking about her love life, 'I don't know why, but I've had a terrible time with relationships,' she confided. 'I either seemed to be on my own for ages or I meet men who are commitment phobics, or who simply treat me badly by lying or cheating on me. I was on the point of giving up when I met my old friend Molly and she told me what to do.'

Pip went on to explain that Molly told her to write a list of what she wanted in a man and to be very specific. Pip wrote her list, and stated that she wanted her man to be someone who made a difference to the world and who was kind and sensitive. The list went on and on. It was indeed very specific and very lengthy. Other friends had thought the whole thing hilarious, but Molly insisted that this had worked for her and Pip was determined to try this approach in the hope it would solve her problem.

Two weeks later Pip went out for a drink with several friends, who had invited along an old friend who was feeling quite low because he had recently split up with his girlfriend. He was, in every detail, the man Pip had asked the universe to find for her – and soon after they married. I watched them holding hands under the table as we sat down for dinner and noticed the glow of two people who were perfect together.

Before I left, Pip told me: 'There was one other magic ingredient.'

'Oh really?' I asked.

'Yes, you must backdate the list, I made my list on the 1st June and so I wrote 1st January that year at the top. This is what brings it into the "now" and makes it happen quickly.' Now I was intrigued. Why had Pip's list worked, whereas the lunch group's approach had failed?

Soon after, I met all the girls at their monthly lunch. I told them about Pip. 'Now, girls, I am curious,' I told them. 'I want to know what is on your list'

They all began talking loudly at once, throwing in various points:

'He must not be a commitment phobic.'

'He must not have any children.'

'He must not be poor.'

'Or miserable,' one interjected.

'He must not be stingy.'

'He must not be fat or balding.'

A light went on in my head. 'Ah,' I said, 'now I get it.' They all stopped. I had their attention. 'I was wondering why your list was not working and now I know. It's because you're giving a list of what you do not want in your life. The universe only hears the chunk of words.' I continued to explain, 'If you walk along the street saying: "I do not want to be mugged, I do not want to be mugged," the universe just hears, "I . . . mugged, I . . . mugged" and the mugging energy will flow to you and you will be mugged. That's how it works.'

So to recap, these ladies were attracting either no one, or men who possessed the attributes they didn't want! I asked them all to write down what they DID want. As they began writing their list in the positive (rather than the negative) they settled down, looked happier and backdated their lists.

I haven't seen them for quite a few years now. They stopped meeting every month for lunch. One woman moved to Australia with her new husband, while another moved to Scotland to be with a new boyfriend. They all have met someone and moved on with their lives, all except one who decided to stick with her old list – her choice!

If you are currently looking for love, here is a simple exercise to show you how you can write your own wish list to manifest your dream man or woman.

The Love Wish List

◆ Write your list in your journal and make sure it is in the positive, stating what you really want from a partner.

◆ Once you have your list, feel free to cross bits out, rewrite and add information. You want the universe to be very clear about what you want.

◆ Now jot down what you will do together. Write 'A day in the life of' and really plan out an entire 24 hours from waking up together, tea in bed, watching the news, breakfast, off to work, maybe a Sunday and a leisurely stroll, lunch, movies, to going to bed, having a good night's sleep together (and whatever else you fancy) and waking up the next morning. Plan your perfect day.

◆ Finally, backdate the day you created the list to six months previously.

I told my friend Steve the whole story about the lunch ladies and Pip and the love wish list and he told me, 'I find it a bit hard to believe I could meet a woman with everything I want. I want someone who likes to jet-ski, visit ashrams, watch very old movies and kick-box.' I told him, 'If you send a message to the universe that it is hard to believe, you make it hard to deliver.' He was attaching the energy of 'hard to make happen' to the energy of 'finding love'.

We wrote Steve's list together. Soon Steve met Sue, who loved old movies but was not very fit. She told him, 'I wish I had the nerve to do the things you do.' Over time and with his encouragement she took up his sports and flourished. He said to me recently, 'The only one thing I wish I hadn't asked for on my love wish list is her kick-boxing skills; if I annoy her she can be lethal!'

Using a love wish list is a very clear way to pass your message on to the universe. But sometimes you can manifest your dream partner with just a thought. Remember, 'Thoughts are things' – which my friend Tony Ford discovered.

I've known Tony for over 20 years. He is a man's man: a hard-working builder who enjoys a pint. Many times when we've bumped into each other in the pub, we've had interesting conversations about spiritual matters. As a true Romany gypsy with many ancestors who were fortune-tellers, Tony often has intuitive flashes; but even so I was still surprised when he told me over a drink: 'I manifested my wife.' I prompted him to tell me more as this was a story I had to hear.

'I'd had a tough year,' Tony explained, 'so when a friend of mine won a big sum of money and slapped a ticket to Thailand down in front of me I couldn't wait to go. But once there I found it a difficult place to be. Hard to imagine now because I love the place, but I was worn out and stressed and everyone I had around me there kept making demands on me. Every second of every day someone wanted me to do something, answer something or go somewhere.

'They were also very keen to fix me up with a girl because I'd been single for quite some time. But the girls were either too young, or pushy or simply not my type. One day I distracted everyone by telling them I was going for a nap and I popped out, revelling in some "me" time. As I walked up the road I wondered why I just couldn't seem to meet the right kind of girl for me. It sounds crazy now but I suddenly found myself shouting at the universe, "Why can't you just bring me a nice girl nearer my age, one who is a good person and who laughs at my jokes even when they are not funny." I thought no more of it and went for my walk. Unbeknown to me, I'd put in a request and the universe was about to reply. But not in the way I'd expected. I thought that if anything was to happen it would be there in Thailand, seeing as everyone was so keen to fix me up.

'I returned home and bumped into a girl I was friends with who was from Thailand. We caught up, with me telling her how my trip had gone. After a while she asked me to look after her friend, another girl from Thailand. She told me, "I have to pop out for a couple of hours. Can you show her around?" Reluctantly I agreed, but as Samneang and I walked around I told a terrible joke and she broke into a big smile and laughed. At that point I knew I'd found my girl. We have been together every since. The odd thing is that Sam is from the very part of Thailand I visited when I put in my request.'

Tony went on, 'Another odd twist is that many years ago I had a dream that has always stayed with me. It was nothing much; just that I was looking out of a back door with a broom in my hand.

'Sam and I bought a café together in Langley village, Slough, and one night as I cleared up after the day's work I opened the back door and there was the image I had seen in my dream. Was the universe waiting for me to put in my request to bring me what I had seen all those years ago and my perfect partner? I don't know, but the universe heard me – and here I am.'

I have noticed that often the ideal person for us at that moment in time is not who we expect. One client of mine, Martin, had just divorced for the second time and decided to lick his wounds with a Caribbean holiday. The last thing he expected was to come back with his third wife! Martin told me afterwards, 'In my mind I knew I would meet someone new at some point, but I expected her to be blonde, in her 40s and professional. Instead I am now married to a black girl half my age, who is not a professional.'

How to Spot 'the One'

Over the years I have regularly been asked, 'How do I know if this man/woman is the one?' I have had time to ponder this question and I believe that Cosmic Energy works on a very personal level: if the person you are seeing is the right one, there will be some very obvious clues. Now firstly I would like to say that many of you reading this book may feel as if you are failing if a relationship doesn't last for ever or if you do not meet the right partner quickly, having worked through this chapter. However, it is important to realise that maybe you need to date a few people and gain some life experience before you meet your perfect mate.

Dating can be fun and often you discover what can be right for you by working out what is not right or suitable. Think of it as reverse Cosmic Energy psychology!

Spotting 'the One'

These are key clues that I want you to look out for, the universal signs that tell you if you are with 'the one':

◆ You will become more confident
◆ You will become more YOU!
◆ You will become healthier
◆ You will become luckier

When you are with the right person you do get luckier. You find your career begins to take off, your health improves and opportunities in all areas of your life open up to you.

On the other hand, if you are with the wrong person you will find that you are often tired, you will find yourself worrying and becoming a little paranoid or jealous. Your health will suffer; you may find little things start to go wrong in your life.

Having the right person in your life helps create a flow of Cosmic Energy that enhances all areas of your life.

Case Study

Patrick was convinced he had met the right girl. She was successful, beautiful and well connected. He adored her on sight. He dropped in to see me for a Tarot reading to check on his career and, when I broached the subject of love, he said, 'No need to look. I have met the one.' I always respect my client's wishes and if they don't want to look at a particular area then that is their choice. Before he left I gently said, 'Don't rush into anything. Do have a proper courtship and get to know each other.'

Patrick is not one to take his time with anything, and deep down something niggled me about this girl. Although Patrick was love-struck, he also looked tried and worn and had begun to have business problems. Suddenly people who usually respected him started to ignore his calls and go back on deals.

A short time later, Patrick called to say he had caught his girl-friend with another man. She had been stringing him and another man along to find out who was wealthiest. And her

good connections? They didn't exist. So my intuition was right –
the universe has been sending Patrick signals too, so if this
happens to you (bad luck, bad health, etc.) take notice.

So, now you've found the one, the next step is how to build a
happy relationship.

How to Build a Happy Relationship

Once you have met someone, give the relationship every
chance of working by creating a positive love vibration. One of
the easiest ways to do this is to clear the space in your home.
This will not only create a good impression when your new
partner first comes round to your house or flat but it gets the
energy in your life moving again, raising your love vibration.

If you are not convinced that space-clearing is important then
think about how you sleep when your house, and especially
your bedroom, is a mess. Do you feel settled? Do you feel on
top of things? Attractive and in control of your life? You may
feel argumentative with everyone who comes into the property. In short, a house with stagnant energy is bad for your
health, wellbeing and relationships. But a home with flowing
energy is a sanctuary, a haven in which to spend time with your
loved ones – where your relationships strengthen and thrive.

Space-clearing

The principle of space-clearing is allowing energy to flow. Once
you have a good flow of energy in your home you will feel
lighter, clearer-minded and happier. If you visit the home of a
depressed or lonely person you will find a mass of stagnant

energy and most of this will be created by clutter, junk, dust and grime.

By clearing your space you will find more abundance in your life. Here is a four-step plan to restore harmony and connect you with the Cosmic Energy in your home.

1. First, have a really good clear-out. Ask yourself this: if you won the lottery tomorrow, how many items would you throw away? Most people say they would discard a vast amount of their possessions, showing that those possessions are kept because of fear. The spare pair of shoes, the old jumper – so much of it is 'just in case'. If you knew you had the money to buy anything you needed you would not feel it essential to hang on to so much. I want you to walk around your own home, look through drawers, under your beds, in your cupboards, and see how much you would throw away if you became very rich tomorrow – then get rid of it.

    As you walk around your home after you have ditched your junk you will feel lighter. You have taken the first step in creating a wonderful flow in your home. Having junk and too many possessions blocks you from doing things, from having a life and having fun. Clutter robs you of time, space and peace of mind. It creates confusion and low self-esteem.

2. The next step is to clean everywhere: open all the windows and doors, then vacuum, dust and wash, preferably with a neutral-smelling, eco-friendly cleaner. Clean everywhere possible and do not be afraid to use plenty of water and give everything a damn good wash. Dust especially seems to collect negativity. Bad energy hangs on to it.

3. Energise your home. Throughout this book you will find lots of ways to use colour, sound and smell to create a wonderful space. Just decide on the effect you would like, maybe a peaceful haven, or a party pad. Once you have decided on the vibration you would like, simply choose the ingredients for your room spray from the Bach Flower Remedies (see pages 45, 46), and the colours and music to fit your need (see pages 80, 82).

    Problems arise when we have stacks and stacks of items, such as layers of unwanted gifts going back ten, twenty or more years. Instead of carrying a positive message they block our flow of energy, keeping us stuck in the past.

Case Study

A friend of mine, Tom, loves to keep everything he is ever given. He began to realise that his life was not progressing, so he decided on a clear-out.

Tom is gay and has had many of his close friends and an ex-lover die from Aids. He could not bear to throw away the cards and notes they had sent him over the years. His home was almost like a shrine to his dead friends. Deep down he knew it was wrong to keep their possessions around him, but he was doing it because he was trying to keep their energy alive.

Tom decided to put most of his possessions into storage and have just a few items from the past around him. Every so often, he would take the current range down and put it into storage, then bring something else out. This meant he could connect with the people who had passed over in a fresh way – just as you do when you unexpectedly come across a forgotten Christmas card or trinket from someone, which reconnects you to them.

Tom also began to display images and ideas of what he wanted in his life: his ideal home, partner, work, his hopes and dreams went on the wall above his dining room table. He realised that he needed to build his own life as a tribute to those who had departed.

Colour

Now you have cleared your space, I want to turn to colour. Colour is such a powerful mood-creator, but it is often overlooked concerning relationships. But did you know that major paint manufacturing companies employ colour psychologists to advise on the use of colour and its psychological properties? This aspect of the business is taken so seriously that months are spent planning each new paint collection and deciding on the colour combinations to show in brochures and other marketing materials.

I do realise that you may not be able to redecorate your entire home to build a better relationship, so there are two ways you can use this information. You can either use it to pick out new paint colours for key areas in your home, or use the same colours in accessories like cushions, flowers, candles, rugs, curtains, throws and even light bulbs. Don't worry – just introducing some of the right colours will have a beneficial effect on building a happy relationship.

Look over the following colours to decide the effect you require to help you boost your relationship in a particular area.

- ◆ Red: Brings passion and heightened sensuality; do not use if you have been arguing.
- ◆ Pink: Encourages love and romance.
- ◆ Green: A good choice if you want your partner to spend longer with you regardless of how busy he/she might be at work. Green will help him relax, rather than rushing off.
- ◆ Blue: If your partner is feeling uptight, this will relax them.
- ◆ Maroon: This colour has a powerful effect, so use it if you want them to take you and the relationship seriously.
- ◆ Peach: Connects gentle feelings with passion. I have suggested this to clients who feel their suitor is more interested in sex than love.
- ◆ Black and silver: These colours give a feel of sensuality and intelligence.

Aroma

Rose stimulates love but for a really special evening, use patchouli or musk. These aromas heighten feelings of sensuality and passion. You can burn candles containing these aromas or make up a love spray (see page 67).

You can also use your love spray for new and existing relationships. A good way to use a love spray is to squirt it a few times in a room before your partner comes home, or comes round. Good Bach Flower Remedies for building relationships are:

- ◆ Vine: Brings unconditional understanding between you, your partner and your extended family. Has an energy that creates the ability to live and work alongside others in harmony.

◆ Rock water: Opens up the heart and allows joy to enter.

◆ Mustard: Creates an inner peace that nothing can shake.

Sound

'If music be the food of love, play on,' said William Shakespeare, and nothing is more true. People often use music to create an impression as a way of saying who they are. Notice how many people wear a T-shirt with the name of a musician or band on it. They want the world to know they are a goth, or into hard rock or hip hop or whatever. It is a big mistake to make this statement to someone you hardly know, or want to impress. If you advertise a type of music they do not like, it builds an immediate barrier.

Try to discover what your guest likes in the way of music. Play something that has good lyrics. So many songs have negative lyrics; these words go straight into the subconscious mind, uncensored. Be careful what you plant into the minds of your suitors and partners!

Music can reduce someone to tears or make them smile in an instant. It is one of your most potent tools, but do use it wisely and effectively. It can create a vibration instantly.

Overcome Conflict With a Lover

It is lovely to think that romance is like it is in the movies – two people meet and live happily ever after. In reality, modern-day life is full of stresses and situations that can put pressure on even the best of relationships.

People work long hours, can suffer from financial worries and have ex-partners or family who interfere in their lives. Step-children or elderly parents can also create extra stress. All these problems are solvable, but at times you can be your own worst enemy, letting your imagination go into overdrive and letting your fears create problems that don't exist. Because your partner often works late or is tired, for example, you may start to feel they are going off you. Or you may be the overly busy one, and not have the time or money to treat your partner as you did at the beginning of the relationship. In other words, the cosmic love vibration that was so high when you first met has dipped a little. This is natural enough as you settle into a regular life together, but from time to time you will want to give that vibration a lovely boost and clear away any little problems or stresses that could possibly grow into something much bigger if left unchecked.

Your own Etheric Energy (the energy that is part of your outer aura) can build a bridge to your loved ones and create a wonderful flow of Cosmic Energy.

In my book *Instant Intuition* I introduced Etheric Energy Techniques, and I have explained how Etheric Energy works in Chapter 2 (see pages 33–5). Over the years I have been astonished at how when a client is talking about someone they used to love but have not heard from in some time, that very person calls them while they are with me. This has happened many times. I began to realise that somehow they were picking up our vibes, our message, our Cosmic Energy that they somehow connected with – despite the physical distance between us.

I began experimenting, and used various Etheric Energy Techniques – EETs – to connect to old friends that I had not seen for some time, clients and even famous people I didn't know but wanted to meet. Again, the results were astonishing. Over and over again, the phone would ring, or someone would contact me and invite me to an event the celebrity would be attending. It was as if the message was connecting on a very real and deep level.

Since *Instant Intuition* was published, many people have contacted me to report how they have used EET to tap into the thoughts and feelings of people all over the world: people they love but do not understand, their children, partners and also their bosses or mothers-in-law. The results have been outstandingly accurate and immensely helpful – and this technique can be particularly effective in overcoming love problems.

You are now about to take a giant leap forward with EET. You will learn how to use EET to overcome the earthly part of us that gets in the way – our hang-ups, or reservations, our fears and blocks. EET sends energy directly to where you want it to go. It is pure and without prejudice. The only motive is good honest love.

You can use an Etheric Energy hug (see page 86) to calm a situation that has got out of hand, such as an argument or dispute that has escalated. You can use it to connect with a loved one when they are being defensive or difficult to talk to. You can use it on anyone, from a difficult neighbour to your partner or child or best friend. By giving someone an Etheric Energy hug they will 'feel' a wonderfully positive love vibration from you and will forget about any negative feelings they may have. You will see their barriers come down and they will become much more reasonable.

The following story is a good example of how an Etheric Energy hug can be used regarding relationships. A client of mine, Troy, had been married before and had been heartbroken when his wife left him for her boss, taking their tiny daughter with her. Soon Troy's ex moved from their native country of America to Sweden where her boss had a new posting.

Troy managed to get a transfer to London and regularly travelled to Sweden to see his daughter. While living in London, he met Gemma. They fell in love and married after just three months. After a few years I could see there was a strain around them both. Troy came to see me first, telling me, 'Gemma seems to be quite sulky these days. I try to talk to her but she won't tell me what is wrong. We have both been working hard to save up for a house, but apart from that I do not have a clue what is bothering her. I do hope she is not going off me.'

I taught Troy how to send Gemma an Etheric Energy hug. A short time later, Gemma popped in for a consultation. She told me how Troy's ex-wife had separated from her boss and was now in regular contact with Troy. She was concerned that he still had feelings for her. And, 'To top it all, when I mentioned having a child to Troy, he simply said, "Not just yet," and changed the subject.'

I never get involved personally in a couple's conflicts – but what I can do is give them the tools, such as the Etheric Energy hug, to help them overcome the issue. In this instance Gemma felt she was living on a knife edge, so I asked her to send Troy an Etheric Energy hug. She had tried to talk to him about his ex but he had just changed the subject, leaving an awkward silence.

Gemma sent Troy an Etheric Energy hug every day and soon he began to open up and tell her how he was being polite to his ex because he needed to know her plans and if she was thinking of moving back to America. He also told her that he now wondered what he had ever seen in the woman; he could see she was a hard and cold person.

As they began to open up they both continued to send each other Etheric Energy hugs (without realising each other was doing it) and as they talked Gemma told Troy her fears. He was astonished that she had been threatened and worried. She then told him about her concerns – about his reaction to the subject of their own children. Again, Troy was stunned. He explained that he simply wanted everything to be perfect for their child and wanted to get it right this time.

That night they arranged a second honeymoon in the same place as their first. I have a feeling it will not be long before they have their house and a child of their own. I wonder if they ever told each other about the hugs they had sent. I certainly haven't mentioned to either of them what the other is doing.

Now, I am going to show you exactly what Troy and Gemma did and how you can send someone you love an Etheric Energy hug. Etheric hugs can be sent to anyone close to you, or someone you need to connect with – your child away at university who is struggling, an elderly person living alone, someone difficult who will not talk to you, and even a friend you have fallen out with and want to smooth the way so you can pick up your friendship.

....

How to Send an Etheric Energy Hug

Allow yourself plenty of time for this exercise and make sure you will not be disturbed.

1. Begin with the opening up technique on page 23.

2. Now spend time focusing on the person you want to send the hug to. Visualise their face, their smile, and take time to run through times you have spent with them – especially the good times. Put in as much detail as you can. Imagine their voice, even their smell. Remind yourself of things they have said, their laugh and the way they walk and sit.

You may find it easier to have photograph or even a video of the person in front of you. If you have a message from them on your phone answering machine or have them recorded somewhere, this will all help build a complete picture. You can also hold an item of theirs or something they have sent you.

3. Now focus on your aura. Allow it to become bigger and brighter – make your aura really shine and spread out further and further. Now become aware of the outer edges and allow them to spread out, becoming longer and longer just like arms.

4. Imagine that the recipient is in front of you. Imagine wrapping your Etheric Energy around them. Feel all the good feelings you have ever felt about this person flow down into the arms and surrounding them through your hug. Send love and happiness to them. Keep focusing on any good thoughts, times and feelings you have shared with them. Again, allow this energy to flow down and surround them.

5. Now feel all the good feelings mingle with your own Etheric Energy and wrap right around them.

6. Spend as long as you wish on your Etheric Energy hug. Then when you are ready, give them a final squeeze then pull back your Etheric Energy and aura back to their normal size, shape and colour.

7. Carry out the closing down technique on page 24 to finish.

Go about your everyday business and let the universal energy get to work.

Rekindle a Romance from the Past

Helena is one of my favourite clients. She is the mother of four daughters, and has a very difficult and cold husband. Her husband was often away on long business trips, sometimes for weeks on end, and we both had a strong feeling he had a secret life and a mistress. He was also a drunk and a bully. Over the years I hoped Helena would leave him, but she is a dedicated mother and, like many men of his ilk, he totally controlled the finances and hid every penny. If she left him, she and her kids would struggle. She didn't mind for herself, but she didn't want her girls to suffer.

In 1993 a man called James crossed her path and there was an instant attraction. Helena is very proper and for two years she and the chap met for a coffee and never went beyond a flirty glance. Over time this grew into more until they were crazy about each other.

The trouble was, Helena could not live with herself; even though she knew her husband was committing adultery she could not bring herself to continue with this emotional affair, so she ended her friendship with James.

After a few months she called me and said, 'Anne, you have to help me get James back. I miss him so much.' I went to see her and we looked at the Tarot cards. I could see that James missed her as much as she missed him. We sent over some love energy and the very next day he called her.

Now they were back on track, but three times over the next three years Helena finished her love affair with James because she felt so guilty. Each time she called me up, we sent James an Etheric Energy hug and each time he called. The final time was in 1995 and I told her, 'If you finish with him this time, you will lose him for ever.'

Some months later Helena was beside herself with grief. She had called his mobile number, but it was a dead line. She called his home, but he'd moved and the new occupant didn't know where James was now living. She called the company he worked for and they told her he'd changed job and they had no idea where he had gone. Helena resigned herself to the fact she would never see him again. There was no way of contacting him. That was it – she had finally blown it.

Helena never forgot James, and several months ago she contacted me again. She asked, 'I know it has been a while, but can you help me get him back?'

I told her, 'Helena, it has been eleven years – it's a bit of a long shot.' I could hear the sadness in her voice and I knew she deserved more than the life she had, now her daughters had left home. Things were no better with her husband, either, and she had just recovered from a serious illness.

Together we sat in her front room; we connected with our Etheric Energy then together we sent James a massive hug. We sent him every bit of energy we could muster.

Three days later he called her, after eleven years. Helena left me a message but she was so excited I could hardly understand what she was saying. Yet the joy in her voice told me they were back on track.

'This time, don't let him go,' I told her.

'Believe me, Anne, I won't, thank you so much,' she said.

How to Break Free From a Past Love

But what if you are not looking for love but actually want to escape it? What if you want to break free from a lover for good? Petra is a good example of someone with this love dilemma.

In her own words, she was a doormat. She had been seeing

this particular man for many years and would sit by the phone hoping he would call. He would pick her up then ignore her for weeks. I had told her previously that this was going nowhere but she could not seem to break loose.

On one occasion she had been particularly distraught because she had found a woman's phone number on his mobile that he had been calling repeatedly. She listened to his answerphone messages while he was in the bath. She told me, 'I know it is wrong, but I couldn't help myself.' The mystery woman had left a message saying what a fantastic night they'd had and thanked him for the gift. Petra had not received one gift from him in over seven years. She was heartbroken.

I encouraged her to be firm and leave him but all she would say is, 'Will he still want me?'

I decided to try Thought Field Therapy (TFT) on her to release the heartbreak. I asked her how upset was she on a scale of one to ten, with ten being as bad as she could possibly feel and one being not bothered at all. She said eleven – and was deadly serious. I got her to tap on the key energy points for releasing love pain. When she tapped I could see her features soften, her eyes brighten. I kept her tapping, watched her shoulders relax, and saw the glimpse of a smile. I asked her, 'On a scale of one to ten, how do you now feel about this man?' She said, 'I am not so bothered now. How strange.' We kept tapping until she was down to number one.

The following day she called me and said, 'Oh my God, what have you done to me?' I was concerned and asked her what had happened. She said, 'I cannot believe I was brave enough to do this, but he called and asked me to go over to his house. As usual, he expected me to drop everything and jump into bed with him. I told him I was busy. I could hear the shock in his voice. I told him I didn't appreciate the way he treated me; I told him he was a liar. I then told him it was over and I booked myself a wonderful holiday in a luxurious resort. He had promised me a holiday for seven years and now I was going to take it without him. It's finally over, and finally I feel free to move on with my life.'

I had known Petra for over twenty years and I could hardly believe what I was hearing. Today she is still strong and any time she gets a wobble about anything at all, she simply taps and away it vanishes.

This is the algorithm I use for love pain. It will work on any upset or trauma.

Tap Away Love Pain
This tapping sequence, or Trauma Algorithm, comes from Roger Callahan's book, *Tapping the Healer Within*. It's the technique I used to help Petra, and the one I use most on clients with love pain.

....

Trauma Algorithm

◆ Think and focus on whatever it is that is upsetting or stressing you. Allow the feeling of upset to surface.

◆ Rate your distress level on a scale of one to ten, with ten being the worst you could possibly feel and one being no trace of upset at all. Write down your rating.

◆ Using two fingers of one hand, tap a spot at the beginning of your eyebrows, just above the bridge of your nose. Tap five times, firmly and gently – not nearly hard enough to bruise, but solidly enough to stimulate the energy flow in the system.

◆ Tap the 'collarbone' point. To locate it, run two fingers down the centre of the throat to the top of the centre collarbone notch. This is approximately where a man would knot his tie. From there, move straight down an additional 2.5 cm (1 in), and then move to the right another 2.5 cm (1 in). Tap this point five times.

◆ Take a second rating and write it down. With the vast majority of people it would have decreased by at least two points. I usually tap on these two points until the rating is as low as one or two.

....

Creating Your Own Love Remedies

I have used a wide variety of the techniques and remedies with my clients over the years. When choosing your own remedies, use your instincts and go with those that feel right. You may be drawn to certain ingredients (they may jump out of the list at you) or you find that one of the descriptions resonates with exactly what you are feeling right now.

As I've outlined in this chapter, there are various ways that you can use love remedies. Here's a summary:

1. Create a love spray choosing Bach Flower Remedies and essential oils (see the aroma section in Chapter 2, page 42).

2. Drink a love remedy. Add two to four drops of Bach Flower Remedies to a glass of mineral water and drink it.

3. Make a crystal elixir. Cleansed crystals are placed into a glass of mineral water, and the crystal water, or elixir, is then drunk. Always check that crystals are safe to use as elixirs – some are not recommended. Also, it is not safe to make an elixir for someone without their knowledge.

4. You can also put essential oils in a bath and bathe in the water – alone or together. Again, check that the essential oils you want to use are safe to use in bath water – some oils cause sensitivity. Other oils are not recommended during pregnancy. Lavender is a deeply relaxing oil for bath time – add a few drops to the bath water after you have run the bath and disperse the droplets in the water.

The Mystic Mountain

In Chapter 2 I told you about a wonderful mystic mountain I visited at Alladale in Scotland. The mountain connected me to everything in the universe and the world. As I stood on top of the mountain I knew that any time I needed anything, all I had to do was connect with that energy and I could access whatever I needed. Below is a mystic mountain visualisation to help you connect with all the love in the world. When you can feel the love around you, this feeling helps you reach out and find the love of someone next to you.

....

Mystic Mountain Visualisation

Allow special time for this exercise. It is very powerful – it boosts your love vibration and leaves you with a wonderful glowing feeling.

◆ Begin with the opening up technique on page 23.

◆ Find yourself a comfy place to relax, close your eyes and allow your breathing to deepen.

◆ Imagine yourself to be out in nature walking through a field of long grass on a warm and sunny day. Up ahead you see a beautiful tall mountain glistening in the sunlight. This is the most beautiful mountain you have ever seen. It seems to have energy and a life of its own. It is as if the mountain is welcoming you and smiling at you.

◆ Walk up to the base of the mountain and notice a steady path winding upwards to the top of the mountain. As you look up, notice that the peak is among the clouds.

◆ At that moment a cloud gently floats down and settles beside you and carries you up the mountain. As you gently float up and up you feel the air becoming cleaner and purer. The air has become so sweet and so pure that you feel at peace. Your mind now has complete clarity. Enjoy the feeling of peace with the world and the universe and know that everything will always be just fine, just as it is.

◆ You are now reaching the top of the mountain. Jump off the cloud and stand on top of the mountain. You look to the east and see a huge city bustling with activity. You look to the west and see the sea; you watch as ships roll in and out of a port. You look to the south and see farms and villages. You look to the north and see a large train station and airport.

◆ As you look in each direction, you feel connected to the world in all its aspects. The hustle and bustle of everyday life and industry, the beauty of the countryside, the sea, so vast and so beautiful; the richness that travel to all parts of the globe brings to our lives. You look up at the sky and wonder at its hugeness and know that beyond the sky is the universe, infinite and so powerful. At that moment you feel connected to the earth beneath your feet, and to the air you breathe and the water you drink, you feel connected to the universe and all its mystery. You feel connected to all the people and abundance and love there is.

◆ Wherever you look there is love, there are couples in love. Parents who love their children, people who have been friends since childhood. There are people who have just met and those who are celebrating their anniversaries. Glance around over seas, over the countryside, over industrial towns, factories, offices, hospitals. Be aware of how much love there is in everyone's heart.

Everyone at some point has experienced love and many people are feeling love at this very moment. Connect to all the love in the world. The old lady who loves her cat, the young boy who loves his horse. A baby has just been born, bringing love and joy to an entire family. Soak up all the feelings of love in the world. Know that the world itself loves you and everyone on her. Soak up through your feet the love the world has for you.

◆ From above feel the love of the universe, the timeless love
that has been there for you in each and every lifetime, in
between lives and in future lives, pure unconditional love.
Connect with all the love that has ever been and that is here
right now and all the love that will ever be. As you connect
feel that love is flowing to you into your heart.

◆ Now send that love straight back out and spread it around
the world. Feel love for everyone and everything. Now feel it
flow straight back. You are now connected to all the love in
the world.

   Every day, send love out and feel it come back – your love
vibration will soar. As your love vibration soars so will your
ability to attract the right person. If you are in a relationship
it will help things rebalance if you have been arguing or
feeling distant from your partner.

◆ Carry out the closing down technique on page 24 to finish.

....

And Finally ...

If your love life is strong, you feel strong. Love is often the
emotion that creates the best and worse times in your life, but
using the techniques in this chapter will help you to ride the
storm and get your life back on track. I suggest you practise and
adapt them for all kinds of relationships, including those with
family and friends.

In the next chapter we will be looking at wealth and abundance. While love is vital to our happiness, we also know the
old saying, 'You cannot live on love alone.' By learning to create
wealth, we can remove one of the biggest pressures on our lives
and relationships.

CHAPTER 4

Creating Wealth and Abundance

Many people of my generation have parents who grew up during the war. Brought up to expect hardship and lack in their lives, from birth they have been blighted with negative wealth vibrations. As a result they subconsciously repel wealth and therefore always struggle with money. But these negative wealth vibrations don't just affect the older generation – anyone from a background where money was tight will be affected by this energy.

Over the years, several events have led to breakthroughs in this area, and I have also worked with many amazing mentors who helped me overcome what I now call 'poverty conscious-ness'. In this chapter I will share with you the manifesting techniques that have worked for me. We will focus on three main issues surrounding wealth:

1. How to attract and create wealth

2. Easy ways to grow your wealth

3. The Cosmic Energy rules for protecting wealth

Before we go any further I want to define 'wealth'. Wealth is not just about having money – there are plenty of people in the world who have more money than they need, but they still feel poor. And there are plenty of people who have less money than the majority, who feel rich. Wealth is relative. It is a feeling of abundance, of enjoying what you have and watching it grow. It is about belief, and knowing that you can draw to you exactly what you want and need. The belief that you deserve to have abundance in your life.

Once you believe you deserve wealth it will flow to you in the way of hard cash but also assets such as property, shares and money in the bank that grow and grow.

Wealth is another facet of Cosmic Energy and when you tap into this energy, your abundance will grow.

The following exercise will give you a true picture of how you feel about wealth on a subconscious level before we tackle those three important topics – creating, growing and protecting wealth.

Test your Cosmic Wealth Barometer

Answer the following questions as honestly as you can:

◆ If tomorrow you lost everything you own, how confident are you that you would recover and get back on your feet?

◆ Do you feel that part of your life path is to struggle, to be comfortable or to be very rich?

◆ Do you feel you have something to offer that is worth paying for?

◆ Do you feel resentful towards those who have more than you?

◆ Did you hear negative comments about money when you were growing up?

◆ If so, do you feel it affects you now?

◆ Can you imagine yourself never, ever worrying about money again?

◆ Do you feel being wealthy would present you with any problems?

◆ Finally, how would having thousands, or millions, in the bank change you?

Look over your answers and see how your beliefs are affecting your wealth vibration. You may be unconsciously sabotaging wealth by creating problems that eat up your money as soon as it is earned. Or you might be attracting 'takers', whom you let spend your money for you (friends who never have any money so you pay for them; or a partner who relies on you financially because they think you won't say no). The good news is that you will find the solutions to these wealth problems here in this chapter.

How to Attract and Create Wealth

When you think of it, money is simply bits of paper or little round pieces of metal; years ago it was bags of salt. It's simply the value we give to it. A number of countries like Zimbabwe have had their money devalued from being worth a great deal to virtually nothing overnight.

It is vital that you see money as a positive force, something that puts food on the table and a roof over your head. It can solve your problems and give you a great life.

As you work your way through this chapter you will discover some of the associations and feelings you have to do with money, and you will be able to change any unhelpful ideas into seeing money as a dynamic and positive force in your life.

The Energy of Money

Many people go through life being afraid of money – afraid they will not have enough or that they will lose the cash they have at present. Because money is so important to our survival, everyone has very strong beliefs about it. You transmit your energy onto money, and that energy helps ensure that whatever beliefs you hold about money are manifested. So if you think you will never have enough money, this is the message you send out to the universe. And this fear becomes your reality: remember, 'Thoughts are things.' On the other hand, if you expect to always be comfortable and affluent you will be, so it's vital to see money easily flowing your way, growing and creating wonderful energy in your life.

Masters of Manifestation

Through my work I meet many people with fascinating stories, and the subject of manifesting often comes up. Many people are good at manifesting JUST enough. They will tell you how their electricity bill came to £135 and guess what? They won exactly £135. And yes, this is an amazing thing to be able to do and it demonstrates the power of manifestation (to be able to get the exact amount you need or near enough is astonishing). But I have to ask, while you are doing this manifestation, why not add a couple of zeros on the amount?

Spiritual people often block themselves from being wealthy. Somehow they seem to believe that they are not worthy if they are rich and that having wealth and a decent life is shallow. But I truly believe that if you have money you are not shallow and if you are reading this book about Cosmic Energy (and are spiritually developing) then you will want to make the world a better place. You are not the type of person to walk past an elderly woman who has fallen over in the street, are you? You try to do your best and if you have money, trust me – you will do good things with it and you will be happier. I struggled financially for a fair bit of my life and I can honestly say it blocked me from really getting on with my work and from helping others. Having money in your pocket means that if someone close to you needs medical help you can pay for it, if a child needs extra education you can pay for it. In fact, any time you see someone with a problem you can provide the help they need.

You also free yourself up when you stop struggling. You cannot reach your full potential while you are working all hours to make a small amount of money and just about survive. If money flows to you then you can study, you can pay for whatever you need to fulfil your destiny and help others. The best manifestors I know do give a hand up to others along the way.

But how do you really feel about allowing yourself to receive good things in life? For instance, how do you really feel about paying £500 for a pair of handmade shoes – which have not been produced in a sweat shop in China? Now bear in mind that having this type of spare cash means you are not hurting anyone and it does not take anything away from anyone else. When I ask this question, most people flinch; the thought of having such an expensive pair of shoes makes them feel uncomfortable. But being poor doesn't make you a more worthy person. It is a way of devaluing yourself. You need to allow yourself to receive and to have a good life.

Many of my friends can be so specific with their manifesting that it's mind-boggling. Clare, Carmen and Jude all have the ability to combine leading spiritual but fabulous lives. They all believe that the world is abundant and good things are here for us to enjoy.

Clare's Story

First, I will tell you about Clare, she can manifest both big and small things. A couple of years ago there was an expensive handbag all the London girls were after and only a few were made. Clare wanted one of these handbags and decided to manifest one. Her friends shook their heads as they told her there were none left for love nor money.

Clare rang every shop that was liable to have one but was told repeatedly, 'I'm sorry, we're sold out.' However, she knows that you can manifest anything and on a flight to New York for business she worked on manifesting that handbag. On arriving in the Big Apple she went to a mall to pick up a couple of things and there in a shop window was the bag. Now let me stress the bag was just as elusive in New York as it was in London, yet there it sat proudly in the window. Clare walked into the shop and asked, 'Is that what I think it is?' The shop assistant was beaming from ear to ear and said, 'Oh yes, we have been waiting for someone to notice. We don't know how we came to overlook it but we just found one out the back. And you are such a lucky lady.' Five minutes later, Clare walked out of the shop with her manifested 'it' bag.

The next day Clare travelled from New York to Los Angeles. As she sat on the plane watching a movie she thought how gorgeous the main actor was and how fabulous it would be to meet him. He is now a household name having just starred in one of the biggest movies of the year.

She thought to herself, 'I want to manifest meeting this man.' I promise you faithfully that when Clare arrived at her hotel in Los Angeles her travelling companion said, 'Have you just seen who has arrived?' In the hotel reception was the very actor she had decided to manifest. That afternoon he sat down on the sunbed next to her and began chatting. Later that week they went on several dates. From making the decision to actually meeting this hunky film star took exactly three hours.

Clare's travelling companion said, half-jokingly, 'If you can manifest that well, why don't you manifest me a television show in America?' Within two weeks he was offered a major deal with a big TV network.

Last year Clare decided she wanted to date her heart-throb, a major pop star and one of the most eligible single men in the world. Very soon they seemed to be virtually joined at the hip. I asked Clare what she did to manifest him and she told me, 'I used to have a small photo of him and I would regularly focus on it when I wanted to connect with him. I then visualised a bridge between my heart and his heart.'

Clare also played his music to enhance the connection. When I asked her what tips she had for would-be manifestors she told me, 'I think belief is a big part of it. Look for evidence it's happening, even small. It helps build up confidence and belief that it's working. Also know that if you do not get what you want, it's because it would be to your detriment.'

Clare has manifested for years. She has built up her manifesting skills and energy and has manifested the lifestyle that created the opportunities and situations to put her in the right places at the right time. You may want to start with something a little easier then increase gradually. By manifesting smaller things you will build your confidence and abilities, ready to build up to bigger items. Don't start at the million-pound home. Feel free to put the idea out there to get the ball rolling, but still be working on the smaller stuff – the step along the way to the bigger dream.

Top Tip

Many of the best manifestors I know have a manifesting space on a wall. They put in this space their dreams and wishes, they place pictures of things they want and places they wish to visit. They invariably get what is on their wish wall. Others have a scrapbook of their dreams.

Carmen's Story

Many years ago when my friend Carmen was airline crew she didn't have much money, but all the same she put together a folder of her dream home. She put in pictures from magazines of her ideal kitchen, dining room and bathroom. She planned the colours and the materials that she wanted. Whenever she saw a picture for her dream house she put it into her dream home folder.

Last year Carmen walked into an exhibition and immediately fell in love with a painting by a relatively unknown Portuguese artist. She had to have this picture for her dream home that she was about to collect the keys for. (By the way, her dream home even has its own beach!)

Carmen came across her original dream home folder and was amazed how after all these years she had manifested almost exactly what she had dreamt of. As she flicked through her dream home folder, she noticed a tiny picture on the dining room wall of one of the pictures. Something about it looked familiar and so she had the picture enlarged. Imagine how stunned she was to see it was a picture by the same unknown Portuguese artist.

Jude's Story

The final master of manifestation I want to introduce you to is Jude, who believes that we all manifest all the time without realising it. She said to me recently, 'If we realised how much we manifested by our own thoughts we could avoid the bad ones far more.' Jude tends to manifest things she falls in love with, such as her house. She told me, 'There is that determined voice in the back of my mind saying, "I don't want to know how out of reach this is – I just want it." And I always get it.'

Jude wanted a Barista coffee maker; she wanted it so badly she had butterflies in her stomach. She knew it was expensive and 'out of budget' but she didn't give up hope. Then by some strange fate a friend of her daughter bought one by mistake and sold it to her for half the price. Jude got her coffee maker.

Jude believes that if you're desperate and focus on something for too long you can push it away with your own energy. All three believe that to manifest you should focus, then let go and let the universe do the rest.

Top Tips

◆ Have a clear image of exactly what you want. Build up the image in your mind – see the colours, the shape, imagine how it will feel holding the object or walking through the door of your dream home. Get a clear picture in your mind and attach your emotions to what you want to give it more energy.

◆ Bring it into the 'now' and imagine you already have it. See yourself with the 'object' and using it, interacting with it every day. See yourself being with it as natural – you deserve it.

◆ Now let go and let the universe do its thing. After you feel you have built up your manifestation as clearly in your mind as you can, let it go. This releases the energy to the universe. When the time is right, the manifestation will become a reality.

The Magic Mantra

Like most people, I have learnt more from the difficult times than I have from the periods in my life that have been easy. In *Instant Intuition* I mentioned how with two young children I struggled for money like the other young mums in my street.

One day while I was lamenting to Greta my spiritual teacher

about my struggle for money, she told me about a secret mantra. At first I thought she was joking, and then I wondered why she hadn't told me sooner. All I can tell you is this – it works.

This mantra is so effective that I almost baulk at telling you the story because I fear you won't believe me, but if you have stayed with me this far then you will know I have many amazing stories up my sleeve; and they are all true.

I began to say the mantra at first for a few minutes but after a while it became a habit. I chanted the mantra morning, noon and night for two weeks. I said it when I was in the bath, washing up and even walking along the road. I even thought it in my mind when I was in company or watching television. I felt a little daft but continued – to be honest I was desperate for money and I had nothing to lose. For two whole weeks I continued saying the mantra.

Then something amazing began to happen. First, I came home to find a package on my doormat. I opened it and inside was £200. Remember, this was some time ago and £200 was a lot of money then. I had lent this money to an old friend many years beforehand and she had chosen this moment in time to return it, pushing the large brown envelope through my letterbox.

Two days later I won another £200. Bit by bit, money began to come my way. I had a write-up in a newspaper that brought me lots of new clients. I discovered an old book in my loft and sold it for a good sum of money. Within six weeks I was on my feet and moving ahead.

I taught the mantra to a friend of mine, Peter, who had suffered from a run of bad luck. He was self-employed and his business was struggling. Within a short space of time of doing the mantra he was making plenty of money. He told me,

'Whenever I need to bring in more sales I just start chanting — and boy, do they come in.'

Over time I came across other people who used the chant and I even met a woman who chanted for a fur coat to wear for a special occasion. I was truly astonished when, within 48 hours, someone gave her a fur coat. I could understand that someone who was struggling would be helped by the universe to pay their bills, or someone needy something worthy would get it — but a fur coat to wear at a party? It didn't make sense to me, but the positive energy of the chant does not discriminate.

Since I first found success with this mantra, I have met people who have chanted for a new carpet, to lose weight, improve their health or to meet the person of their dreams.

At the time Greta told me about the mantra I just thought it was some magic words that brought you money. I didn't realise there was a lot more to it until a number of Buddhists came to see me and bit by bit they told me the meaning of the chant.

The chant was devised by a 13th-century Buddhist monk by the name of Nichiren. He called it 'the greatest secret of all'. He believed the chant could reach the limits of the universe. He believed it's a normal part of life to wish for things, but along the way we gain enlightenment and we discover what is truly important.

Nichiren believed this was a form of Buddhism everyone could practise and benefit from. He knew that it's hard to be spiritual and reach your highest potential while you are sweating blood about feeding your children; life's worries don't change with history.

....

How to do the Chant

You can do this chant while washing up, cleaning . . . I even do it in the bath. It does bring you what you want – but importantly, as it connects you to the universe, you begin to question what you desire. You still want the nice things in life but you become aware of what is truly important. I have noticed that people like Carmen who use it regularly seem to have an instinctive awareness of the universe and how it works. They naturally see the good in people even when those people behave badly; they are aware of their higher purpose and have a real sense of helping make the world a better place.

The chant reels us in by giving us what we want and need, but then it also gives us a higher awareness as a by-product. A pretty good deal I think. You can also chant for other people. So if you know anyone who's in need, sick or troubled, just focus on him or her and start chanting.

So here we go:

Nam-myoho-renge-kyo
Nam – the 'a' has the sound of the 'a' in father.
Myo – think of it as placing an 'm' before one half of yo-yo
Ho – like the garden implement 'hoe'
Ren – like the bird 'wren'
Ge – sounds like the word get without the 't'
Kyo – similar to 'myo'

Say these words over and over again in a sort of monotone voice, almost a drone. Say them early in the morning for ten minutes or just as you go about your daily business and know that the universe will hear your request.

....

The Wish Box

Another great technique to attract wealth, which you can use alongside the magic mantra, is the wish box. All you need to do is get a box that is special to you, put a few coins in it and money will flow to you.

I gave my friend Charlotte a wish box and showed her how to use it to bring luck and good fortune to her life. She immediately began to do well. She would put into the box a symbol of what she wanted. For example, there was a picture of her ideal car cut out of a magazine, shiny new coins and key words on pieces of paper. Every day Lotty would open the box and visualise what she wanted. One day she called me and said, 'I have stopped using my wish box. Something odd is happening.'

I asked her to fill me in. 'Whenever I use the box I get what I want, but at the same time things seem to go wrong for my husband,' she confided. 'This has happened five times on the trot. I stopped using the wish box for two months but as soon as I put my wishes in the box he had some really bad luck. It seems that when I use the box I get lucky and he gets extremely unlucky.'

Lotty is a smart woman and she pondered why this could be happening. By keeping her eyes and ears open she discovered her husband had been embezzling money from their company. He had forged her signature and stolen money from the company and hidden it in a secret account.

At the time it had looked as if the wish box was working against her husband and making him unlucky, but in reality it had been trying to protect her – and show her that something was wrong in her relationship with her husband. So when the deal he had been working on fell through we knew it was money he had planned to filter away for himself – money that was rightly hers too. It made us both realise just how powerful a wish box can be. By the way, Lotty filed for divorce and dissolved the business just in time. She discovered he had been embezzling money from a number of different sources, and she would have been implicated if she had not left him when she did.

....

How to Make a Wish Box

Your wish box can be made of any material you choose, from wood or tin to woven paper; the main thing is that you like the look and feel of it. Many people use a wooden box because wood absorbs good energy. Also, it's long-lasting, natural and can absorb vibrations from the universe and the earth.

1. If you want something like a car, or a particular style of house, place a picture of what you want in your wish box.

2. Write by hand what you want, fold up the piece of paper and squeeze it in your hand as you visualise yourself with what you want. Squeezing your hand creates a signal. It focuses the energy and intent.

3. Now place on top a stone of your choice. Below is a list of the type of semi-precious stones I have used in the past:

   ◆ Citrine: I also keep a citrine in my purse, it brings a steady flow of money. Europeans visiting South America brought this stone back with them and believed it created wealth; they used to put one into their purse to attract gold.

   ◆ Diamonds: The ultimate money-generator. Even the tiniest sliver will give out the message that you want all the abundance possible.

◆ Emeralds: If you want pure luxury.

◆ Green jade: Brings long-term prosperity. It helps to establish you as a prosperous person without ups and downs in your finances.

◆ Pyrite (fool's gold): This works very well in helping you to get a business thriving. Pyrite helps money flow easily without you always having to work hard for it. This stone gives a lovely buzzy feeling to get you fired and ready for action.

◆ Quartz: Attracts wealthy people into your life, it brings good quality and good service.

◆ I also like to put into the box three Chinese coins, the little ones with the square hole in the middle. They symbolise luck and have centuries of association with wealth and abundance so are good at attracting this vibration.

◆ Also, add anything that symbolises wealth and good luck to you. Many people have a lucky ticket or trinket.

Pop all of these items into the wish box and hide it away. Do always keep your box away from prying eyes – it is personal to you. Each day take out your box and in your hand hold the piece of paper that you have written your wish on. Focus on your wish. Imagine that you already have it.

You can concentrate on one wish at a time or put multiple wishes into your box. The universe will respond to your manifestations just the same.

The Nine Keys to Wealth

You would be amazed at how often people email or write to me and demand that I tell them how they can become millionaires! For some reason, they think I can tell them how to make vast amounts of money drop out of the sky. Now I do believe we can manifest anything we want, but I also believe we are here to work. I truly believe that we are all here for a reason and yes, we are here to learn and grow, but it stands to reason we are here to donate something; to work or do something useful. Yet when I tell this to people they act as if the word 'work' is akin to a swear word.

I constantly meet people who want to contribute nothing to the world but want to be superstars by Wednesday next week. Everyone I know who has done well in life has worked hard. They have contributed and they have put energy into what they do.

Just recently a girl called me who had taken one weekend course in healing. She told me she wanted to write a book, become a high-level teacher and become very famous. I asked her, 'Don't you think you should at least go and heal a few people first?' She hung up on me.

I believe you can be abundant. I believe you can have anything you want, but I truly believe that unless you actually get up and contribute something to the world we live in it is unlikely to happen – or if it does, you will not sustain it. There is a lot of information on manifesting out there, and some people love doing it and find it a great tool. But very few of the people who rave about manifesting are actually wealthy. What tends to happen is they pull off the odd little win: 'I received the exact amount I needed to pay my electricity bill,' or, 'I got a pay rise.' They rarely sustain it.

I believe that if we are working and doing something useful to make the world a better place then we are aligned with our collective higher purpose, and it's a whole lot easier for the universe to deliver. As the old saying goes, 'Money goes to money.' Once you raise your wealth vibration, money will flow your way.

As well as using manifestation, I have spent many years discovering what wealthy people do, and I have realised that there are nine keys to wealth. Many people have one or two of these keys; those with the Midas touch have all or most of them.

Notice how each key will change your vibration and raise it. Each and every time you connect with a person, learn something or put passion into your work, your connection to Cosmic Energy will become stronger and your ability to manifest and work with the Law of Attraction will increase.

Key One: Passion

Put passion into whatever you do. No matter what it is, no matter whether you love or hate it, do a good job. It will raise your energy and when you raise your energy, better things come your way.

Key Two: Keep Learning

Ask, 'How can I better myself? What do I need to learn?' Mediocre people think they know it all and need no help from anyone, especially the universe. People at the top know they need to keep learning and they need luck to succeed. I have never met anyone at the top of their game, no matter what it is, who isn't constantly learning and growing. They look out for new developments in their industry. They listen to other people, even novices. They are never arrogant enough to ignore someone up-and-coming or just starting out.

Ask yourself – what do I need to be learning? Are there any courses I can take? Books I can read? Skills I need to attain so I am able to do my dream work? Whatever lesson or knowledge you need to find out, keep working towards it.

Know your subject; know everything there is to know about your field. Then make your own discoveries and put your mark on what you do.

Key Three: Act as if You Are Already a Success

This is vital; act as if you are already where you want to be. Actually learn to feel what it feels like to be top of your game. As you go about your daily business, act as if you are already where you want to be. If you are driving or sitting in traffic, pretend you are in your dream car, when you enter a beautiful building, perhaps a top hotel, imagine it is yours and all the people there work for you. Imagine your clothes and shoes cost a fortune. Polish those shoes every day and imagine they were hand-made especially for you by the best cobbler in the world.

As you begin to focus on already being a huge success your energy will begin to align to a successful vibration. Opportunities will begin to land at your feet – for example, you could be chatting to someone who puts you in contact with someone else who offers you the perfect business opportunity. Or you may meet an old contact by chance and they make you an offer you can't refuse.

Key Four: Never Miss a Chance

I regularly come across people who tell me how successful they want to be, but when opportunities come along they let them pass.

Recently a young lady came to see me who told me she is desperate to become a famous singer. She takes part in a weekly class and practises at home when she has time. I told her that there was an audition in London that few people knew about, so by going she would have the edge. Before she left me I asked her, 'Do you really think you can make it as a singer?' She looked at me, horrified, but didn't say anything. I told her, 'I have just told you about a major opportunity, an audition for a major West End production that few people know about, but you were about to leave without asking me any of the details. Also when I asked you how often you checked the daily listing of opportunities you told me you rarely had time, yet you also told me you get a full hour's lunch break and you often window-shop.' I didn't want to be hard on her, but unless I pointed this out she would have continued to waste her time.

Whatever your dream – pop star, model, sports star, healer, nurse, doctor, clairvoyant, business owner – you need to be constantly putting energy into what you do. You should be reading about your industry, reading the trade press, making contacts, going to events, networking and taking up any small opportunity, because you don't know where it will lead you.

Key Five: Be Scared of Failure

Fear has energy. Just think what your life will be like if you never attain your dream. How do you feel about that? In workshops I often ask the question, 'Supposing nothing in your life has changed in five or ten years' time. How does that make you feel?' Invariably the participants look horrified.

A few weeks ago I met one of the world's greatest entrepreneurs. He started out in business with a few pounds in his pocket and is now a household name and owns many companies. I asked him, 'Why have you done so much better than most people?' He replied, 'I have worked harder and put in more effort and energy. That is the honest truth. I am not the cleverest person in the world but I put energy and passion into everything that I do. I become almost obsessed with whatever project or deal I'm working on.'

He added that he had a healthy fear of being complacent and when he was starting out had no option but to work hard. 'If I didn't work, I didn't eat,' he told me.

Many people today are simply not hungry enough for success. I know billionaires who are hungry and people living on the breadline who are not. My entrepreneur friend told me, 'For some reason I am always a little bit afraid that I won't succeed. I see that as a healthy sign.'

Key Six: Watch the Company You Keep

Most people's income will be within £10,000 of the five people they mix with the most. So by mixing with wealthier people you increase your own wealth vibration. It rubs off on you. If all your friends are struggling and scratching around for work then this will bring your energy into alignment with theirs. If you mix with people who are doing well your energy will start to vibrate to a more successful frequency. It makes sense, doesn't it? Hanging out with losers will not help you attain your goal.

The Success List

Write down a list of the eight people you mix with the most. Now ask:

◆ What is their income?

◆ How well are they doing?

◆ What is their attitude to wealth and success?

◆ Are they positive in their approach to life, or negative?

◆ When you talk about your aspirations, are they encouraging?

◆ Are they doers or all talk?

◆ Do they tend to get what they want?

◆ Do they sabotage their attempts to get on in life?

Key Seven: Never Make Excuses

Everyone thinks it's harder for them, they're too old or too young, or don't have enough money, or don't have the time, or are too tired. The difference is that successful people find a way. Many of the richest people I know were told at school they would not amount to anything. Five of my richest friends are dyslexics; in a way dyslexic people have an edge because they find another way to do well in life. They seem to push themselves more. As Thomas A. Edison said, 'There's a way to do it better – find it.'

Shakespeare wrote in *Measure for Measure* (Act 1, Scene IV), 'Our doubts are traitors and make us lose the good we oft might win by fearing to attempt.' Old Willie knew about the power of fear, and he was writing in the 16th century. By believing in yourself and putting energy into your goal, you send out a very clear message to the universe – take me seriously. Every effort you make builds momentum until you are a success.

Key Eight: Don't Allow Yourself to Be Badly Treated

If you're in a situation where a boss, customer or contact treats you badly, remove yourself from the situation. If you do not they will take advantage; their poor treatment of you will get worse. Your energy will plummet, and keep plummeting, and you will wonder why your career is not taking off.

Don't think for a second that by sticking around or appealing to their better nature they will change. If you have a bullying boss or clients who treat you badly, move on – get new ones.

I have no problem getting up and walking out of anywhere I do not feel good. I have done this in a dentist's surgery and at dinner parties. Anyone who works with the public knows that the majority of people are lovely but they will also have some stories to tell you about the clients from hell, who are rude and demanding – expecting you to drop everything at a moment's notice. You don't argue with them, you simply don't see them; you tell them you are fully booked for the next ten years. As soon as your refuse to take their appointment your energy will begin to rise. You will feel stronger and a message will go out to the universe that you want good clients.

If you are in a relationship of any kind with a lover, friend, family, colleague or client and they are messing you around or treating you badly, you are allowing your energy to be drained. You must walk away. Walk away when they are in mid-sentence; don't say a word, just get up and go.

Within you is an amazing spark of liberation. When you take control of a situation in which you are being abused your personal power will rise. You may have the urge to laugh – this laughter comes from a feeling of freedom and strength.

People tend to put up with these situations out of fear: fear of being out of work, of getting a bad reference, or not having enough clients to pay the bills. Fear is a huge block to wealth and if you are treated badly, your wealth energy will go on a downward spiral. Negative influences in your life create a chaotic energy field, leaving you tired and despondent – which blocks good and positive people coming into your life.

Key Nine: Build Momentum

Over the years I have met many people who have started businesses that have failed. Often, I see them sabotage their fledgling company by either not putting the energy and time into it to bring in business, or by doing silly things to create problems. Later they will say, 'Oh well, I did my best. I tried.' But did they? Can they honestly say they did their very best to make the business work? Imagine if they lived in the middle of a forest. If they didn't put in the effort they wouldn't eat and their children would die from cold and starvation. Imagine how hard they would work. That is the level of effort and energy that is needed to make a business succeed.

Others will put in a massive amount of effort but will waste energy. They will confuse activity with achievement, by running around in circles. This too is a form of sabotage.

> 'We're busy doing nothing, working the whole day through, trying to find lots of things not to do,' sang Bing Crosby in the film *A Connecticut Yankee in King Arthur's Court.*

In my previous offices in Slough was a media company. They were always rushing around the building saying, 'We are all so busy.' I spent a day with them and they didn't actually do anything at all. They didn't email anyone, or phone anyone or plan anything. They wrote one letter then left it too late to put in the building's post collection and so the boss had to rush to the post office and stand in a queue. The post was collected at 4.30pm each day and they wrote the letter in the morning.

While I was there someone left a message and they didn't pick it up. They were 'too busy'. The call was from a major potential client needing an urgent job done. It would have been their perfect chance to show what they could do. The client went somewhere else.

The amazing thing is that this self-sabotage was lost on them. They were too busy to take the call. I predicted they would soon go out of business, and they did, shortly afterwards.

Many companies came and went in the ten years I was in the Slough office. I noticed that the people who worked late and concentrated hard on where they wanted to be were successful, but the businesses with people who knocked off early because 'things were a bit quiet' or sat playing computer games in between jobs never lasted. Not one of them. It taught me a great deal about priorities.

Successful people put a massive amount of energy and effort into what they do, and they do not stop. Know that the effort you put in is energy, and energy builds. At first you won't see the energy building so you need to have faith and self-belief. You may slave away for quite some time, see the odd customer come along and think things are slow, but if you consistently get your name out there and do a great job you will succeed. The energy will build. It will gain momentum until one day everyone knows who you are and what a great job you do.

By working hard and getting your name out there you are sending out your energy for people to feel by promoting yourself – your name will become known. This is why advertising and PR companies call it 'creating a vibe' or 'a buzz'. They understand that promoting what you do and putting energy into it will create a vibration all of its own that other people will feel; and if the vibe you create resonates with people, they will beat a path to your door.

The same applies if you work for a company. Radio broadcaster Tony James has always advised novice disc jockeys, 'Be your own self-publicist.' Tony has told me, 'When you work in this business you need to let the powers that be know of your successes and how well you are doing.'

Tony is one of the hardest-working people I know, and it reflects back on him. His radio shows are always hugely popular. Time and time again I have seen him take over a struggling programme, yet within a short space of time, the ratings are soaring.

How I Learned About the Abundance Funnel

Even if you follow all the keys to attaining wealth, there will be times when you will need a boost. The abundance funnel is a great way to get money pouring in. By focusing on the funnel you are not looking to raise your income a little or win the lottery – you throw out the message that money from all kinds of sources is more than welcome. It is fascinating to see just how the abundance comes from so many unexpected sources.

Many years ago an old friend, Peter, taught me the abundance funnel. Over time I worked with and refined the technique. I learnt about it after Peter called me up one day and told me he had developed a way of bringing him more business when he wanted it. He told me, 'When I need more clients, instead of spending a fortune on advertising I run one advertisement and do this exercise. Believe me, the phone doesn't stop ringing.'

I've used the abundance funnel, and taught it to many of my clients, for a whole range of things. It works. Why not try it yourself now?

The Abundance Funnel

Get yourself a pen and paper and find a nice spot to sit and relax. You can be inside or outside, sitting under a tree or on a beach, or in your own front room. Sit upright, cross-legged on the floor or ground.

◆ Begin with the opening up technique on page 23.

◆ Close your eyes, sit quietly and spend some time thinking about what you want.

◆ Now open your eyes and write down exactly what you want, really free-flow. Do not stop and think about whether it's possible or likely. Just write it down.

◆ Now focus on the list and imagine what a difference this would make to your life.

◆ You can add to the list at any stage you wish.

◆ Go down your list and put a symbol next to each item to represent it. If you want a car or house you may draw a tiny car or house. For money you may put a pound or dollar sign, or draw a gold coin. For love, you may doodle a heart.

◆ Next, close your eyes and ignore any outside noise and allow your breathing to deepen, as you do so allow every part of your body to relax. Notice how your breathing calms your body and feel this peace flow down to your toes.

◆ Now let the breath flow through your abdomen, up your back and into your shoulders. Still breathing deeply, allow the relaxation to flow into your neck and head, soothing every muscle in your face.

◆ Imagine above you a huge shiny golden funnel, it's so big you could fit four of you inside it comfortably.

◆ Open your eyes and look at your list. Take the first item on the list and focus on the symbol. Now imagine the symbol floating off the page up into the air and into the top of the funnel. Relax and know that the golden abundance funnel is doing its job.

◆ Carry out the closing down technique on page 24 to finish.

One of the most frequent enquiries I receive is from people who run businesses wanting more customers, and the abundance funnel is the ideal exercise to make this a reality. In the past, I have imagined a printed-off email floating into the funnel and lots of new emails requesting appointments floating out of the bottom and landing at my feet. I then imagined answering them and writing their appointments into my diary.

The abundance funnel will bring you an abundance of whatever you ask for and what you need in your life right now.

The Wealth Spray

Cosmic Energy doesn't just work with visualisation. As you know, you can use a whole manner of tools to help – including sprays made up using aromatherapy oils. Personally, I love using a wealth spray. It acts as a magnet, bringing luck and money flowing to you. It's great if you want more or better work. Within seconds of using one I can feel an instant change. My friend Helen has the same results, so whenever we need to boost our finances we spray ourselves, our rooms, our offices and even our computers, purses and chequebooks. I have also made up sprays as gifts for my friends.

Here's how you can make your own wealth spray quickly and simply and, pardon the pun, it won't cost you a fortune.

Making a Wealth Spray

◆ Make up a spray bottle as I showed you in Chapter 3 (see page 67). Use pure spring water and add a few drops of Star of Bethlehem (a Bach Flower Remedy) to clear away any debris from your past that may be blocking you. (You can buy the Star of Bethlehem from Boots and health food shops.)

◆ Oils: I love to use frankincense essential oil ever since I picked some up in Oman. It feels rich.

◆ Crystals: Try pyrite (fool's gold): This stone brings money to us in a solid way. It helps us to build our lives and gives us the abundance to do it with.

◆ Put a few drops of frankincense oil and the pyrite into a jug of mineral water. Stir. Pour off the water into your spray bottle. Then sit holding your bottle and focus on how much better your life will be once abundance flows to you. This will help to energise the water.

◆ Your wealth spray is now ready to use. Spray it around the home to keep wealth flowing in, spray it on your suit when you are asking for a pay rise, spray it onto your hand when you are going to ask for a business loan or a mortgage. You can also spray it around your office, or spray it on you like a perfume before meeting potential new clients or employers.

....

Easy Ways to Grow Your Wealth

Once you have learnt to create and attract wealth, the next step is to make sure your wealth continues to grow by itself. Many of you will have been brought up to think you have to work hard for very penny – yet wealthy people know only too well that money attracts money.

Over the next few weeks, I want you become money conscious – do not spend any money unless you need to. Try to put some money into your savings account every week, even if it's only a small amount. It's a sign that your money is growing. Make sure you are focusing on your wish box too, putting in coins, a £10 or £20 note, and images of how you want your life to be.

Keep an eye out for money; you will find it begins to appear and that unexpected money will come your way. When it arrives, put it into your wish box. This could be finding a penny in the street, down the back of the sofa, or in a pocket. You may also find that you win or are given money. Again, pop it straight into your wish box.

How to Grow Your Money Vibrations

For the next month spend as little money as possible just to get the money vibration growing. It's a bit like putting plant food on your roses to give them a boost. Notice every penny that you usually spend and instead of spending it, drop it into your wish box. Instead of buying an expensive skinny latte take a flask and walk to work if possible. Don't buy any magazines, CDs, DVDs or chocolate bars. Really get the feeling of hanging on to your money and enjoy watching your money grow.

As you become money conscious, you will begin to value it more. A young lady who had just started a business told me, 'I can't wait to spend all the money I am going to make.' I told her that she needed to change that thought if she was to survive in business – money isn't something to get rid of the moment you get it. Two months later she gave up and closed her company. As they say in Hollywood, 'You buy things you don't need, with money you don't have, to impress people you don't like.'

You will never be rich if money burns a hole in your pocket. You need to enjoy watching it grow, and seeing money making more money for you. What is happening on a spiritual level is that the energy of your money is multiplying. And the more money you have, the more money energy will be attracted to you. Once you have surplus money, begin to buy the things you want. Most people do it the other way around – they buy things before they even have the money, which gets them locked back into poverty consciousness. They stop the flow of Cosmic Energy.

Once your money begins to grow, put it into a higher-interest account and start to read up on investing. Remember Key two (see page 114), 'Keep Learning'? While you are reading about money and how it works you are increasing your connection to the energy of money. A good place to start is the money or financial pages of the daily and Sunday papers. Have a money block? Then buy a tabloid, which will explain things simply and in a way you will be able to grasp. Then, once your wealth confidence grows, you can read books and attend seminars on investing and such like.

The Cosmic Energy Rules for Protecting Wealth

Some people are good at making money, but not so good at hanging on to it. This can be a form of sabotage. Have you ever come into money, only to have your car break down a few days later, costing you a tidy sum? Or pull off a great deal or job – only for it to fizzle out? If so, this is section is for you. Even if up until now you have kept hold of your money, this will help you to strengthen that ability and create a stronger link to money energy.

Clearing Money Blocks

Inspirational author and self-help publisher Louise Hay once commented that people get more upset talking about money than they do about anything else. When people come to see me for a reading, money is a main topic – just as much as love, health or work. Yet most people don't have anywhere near the amount they want or need. And even if money does come their way, the first thing they do is spend it.

Watch anyone who wins some money and they will give you a list of their purchases – mostly things they can live without. There is a big difference between someone who has been out of work, or has had a big setback, buying a new washing machine to replace a tired old model and someone who snaps up a plasma television but has nothing in the bank.

So why do people behave in this way? Self-help expert Paul McKenna made a breakthrough discovery while working on his book *I Can Make You Rich*. He realised that most of us are programmed by our past, so if we grew up in a poor background or had parents with poverty consciousness (and constantly said negative thing such as 'Life is a struggle' or 'We're always going to be poor') money would come in one door and go quickly out the other. If you come from such a background you will have those thoughts ingrained in your energy field, creating a downward financial vibration that will result in a lack of abundance. This information was a huge breakthrough for me because although I can make good money – I use all the techniques and they definitely work – I never seemed to hang on to any of it. I told Paul my problem and he showed me how to create an alternate past, meaning you rewrite your own financial history. I found this exercise lots of fun – and it works!

....

Rewrite Your Financial History

♦ Simply close your eyes and imagine that you were born into a wealthy family, one with a positive attitude to money. Imagine how your life would have been if your parents had been rich.

♦ Imagine that the day you were born you inherited a fortune. Focus on how that would have changed you, just knowing you were wealthy.

♦ Imagine you grew up with a healthy attitude to money, knowing that if you needed anything it was there.

◆ How would you have felt? What would your parents have said about money? What presents would you have received? How would life have been different?

◆ Really focus on rewriting your past. Take key times like starting secondary or high school. How different would it have been if you had been wealthy, would you have gone to a private school, had higher aspirations?

◆ Imagine leaving school and going to university knowing that you had plenty of money in the bank.

Every so often focus on this exercise even for a few minutes and add in some more 'memories'. It will strengthen the vibrations.

This exercise cleared my poverty consciousness and enabled me to raise my wealth vibration.

....

Giving it Away

Another way to protect your wealth is tithing, or giving away money. Tithing will make you luckier by raising your vibration and letting the universe know that you are ready to allow the flow of abundance to come your way – and it truly works. Try it out for yourself. Get into the habit of giving. Pop a few coins into a charity box when you are shopping, give good tips for good service, donate things you don't want to your local charity shop. Actually get into the habit of being generous – put your hand in your pocket. Tithing is totally different to frittering money away on things you don't need, wasting money. This is prompted by a desire for material objects from the ego, whereas tithing is prompted by a wish to help others enjoy the abundance vibration.

Many people think that someday in the future when they have more money they will donate something. The universe works in a slightly different way – it wants payment up front. I know several mean people and money rarely comes their way. One old friend deliberately doesn't take enough money when she meets people for lunch. They end up having to pay for her. She never tips and always buys the cheapest of everything. She constantly complains how everyone has got more than her. I suggested she learnt to give a little. She replied, 'No way. I want to make sure I have more than others.' What a shame – she never will have.

Giving creates a flow of wealth energy. When we experience lack, it is simply that our wealth vibration isn't flowing. I have a client who is forever complaining how money never comes her way. In fact she owns several houses and had a good job, but nothing seems to satisfy her. I told her about tithing, and two days later she phoned me to complain, 'I gave a couple of pounds to a charity and I bought my mother-in-law a little gift, but I haven't got anything back yet.' I told her to stop wanting – her constant wants were creating a blockage.

Many of the richest people in the world tithe. According to a BBC news report in June 2006, billionaire investor Warren Buffet donated $37 billion to the Bill Gates Charitable Foundation. Bill Gates was inspired to start the charity by Warren Buffet. Both these men see wealth with a broader vision than most people, which is why they are so wealthy.

The foundation was set up to fight disease and promote education around the world. Bill Gates said, 'There is no reason why we can't cure the top twenty diseases.' Can you imagine having such an aim? I bet both these men sleep well at night knowing they are contributing so much to the world. I know you might be thinking, 'Oh well, it's okay for them,' but every penny you donate has an energy, and that energy carries a stronger energy as it collects with other pennies. Just as one drop of water alone doesn't make much difference, once it joins billions of others it becomes an ocean.

Spread it About a Bit

Andrew Carnegie was the first industrialist to say that the rich have a moral obligation to give away their fortunes. He wrote the book *The Gospel of Wealth* in which he states that once you have taken care of your family you can give away the rest. He built over 2,500 libraries in the world at a time when there was just a handful. In his lifetime he gave away $350 million, according to the Carnegie Corporation of New York.

Tithing can set up an amazing chain of events. About ten years ago a chap called Louis would hang around my local cash point asking people for money as they drew out cash. I would have a quick chat and give him £1. On this particular day the man in the queue behind me said, 'You've just been done. He will spend that on drink.' I told him, 'I have faith in Louis. He is a good man.'

I thought no more of it until about a year later when Louis walked up to me and said, 'You were really kind to me and somehow I began to feel better about myself. I had to go to the hospital later that day and I saw a little old Indian lady in a wheelchair. She was having trouble manoeuvring. So I pushed her outside for a breath of fresh air then wheeled her back inside. About two weeks ago I was sitting outside the cash point and a young Indian lad came up to me and gave me £10. He was her son and he remembered me helping his mother. I have decided not to drink any more – somehow I feel this is a sign not to.' I never saw Louis again from that day. He could be in another town somewhere by a cash machine, but I like to think he isn't.

Never think your little donation or kind word doesn't matter.

Like Louis, we often learn about such things when we're having a difficult time . . . I often meet people who tell me they are unlucky, but luck is simply a form of energy that can go up or down. Gen, a friend I met some years ago when we were both working in the West End of London, discovered this when her luck went on a downward spiral. After she tithed, I witnessed a dramatic turnaround in her fortunes. This is her story.

Case Study

Gen says: 'I am one of those people whose luck has changed for the better, but it hasn't always been like that. A few years ago my luck took a dramatic downward turn and overnight my life fell apart.

One day everything was fine but the next my long-term partner left me for an ex-girlfriend in another country. He simply called and said he wasn't coming home – ever. Apart from suffering the heartache, I also worked for him and so was now out of a job. I could not afford the home we had been renting. Suddenly I had to pack up, find somewhere to live and find a job. I had to rapidly downsize and downgrade my home. I moved in with a friend who a short time later decided to move in with her boyfriend. Again I had to move on.

I then started to work with some friends and they turned out not to be friends at all. They were always late paying my salary and I was even more broke and in debt with the bank – it was awful. Something about being in the depths like that really showed me how easy it is to become very vulnerable and penniless, so I am really appreciative of the position I am now in.

I can remember a time sitting in a café at Waterloo station with a friend. A tramp was trying to steal a sandwich. The manager came over and tried to take the sandwich off him. The old guy just stood there staring at this sandwich and didn't know what to do, and he was shaking. He was clearly malnourished. As I looked at this poor man I could relate to being at rock bottom. At that moment I realised I only had £20 left in the world before I hit my maximum on my credit card and overdraft. I wanted to buy this starving homeless guy his lunch. I had the money in my purse, it was only £5 and I hoped if ever I needed it, someone might come to my rescue . . . and they did.

The girl I was with thought it was really kind of me – I didn't; not only was it necessary for this man to eat something, it was also necessary for me. I needed faith that I'd get help if I needed it, and by helping him it reaffirmed in my mind that people do help one another and you're never completely alone. As it was, the manager wouldn't accept the money from me and let the tramp have his sandwich – so that thought was reaffirmed to me immediately – one good deed started another from someone else like a ripple. This old shaky guy came and thanked me about six times after that and from a purely selfish point of view, I hoped I had helped my own karma too because I needed it!

Suddenly from having to sell most of my belongings, having nothing in my purse, no food on my shelves and even washing my hair in Fairy Liquid (yep, it got that bad), out of the blue help came from an unexpected source. My first boyfriend who I hadn't seen in about fifteen or more years appeared. He helped me move my stuff from London, as I had to move in with my parents until I sorted my life out. He even paid for the truck and the storage of my stuff.

Knowing how anger and bitterness can work against our energy I sent Christmas wishes to the very person who had been the catalyst in this downward spiral – the man who'd left me. I felt pretty low and didn't expect to hear from him. In fact I wasn't looking to hear from him; it was part of my healing process to forgive and move on.

The text opened the floodgates from him. Things had gone badly wrong between him and his ex-girlfriend. Suddenly he felt he could apologise for everything and show his remorse. Within a couple of weeks (and many long phone calls from Australia) he was offering to drop everything and come back to England, and suddenly everything in my mind changed. I decided I would give him another chance. I headed for Australia. I knew it wouldn't be a bed of roses, but I was determined we were going to get over this – and we did.

In a way it's the same for Mike too. After he had left me, he also had a dreadful time and things with the other woman didn't work out almost from day one, apparently. Funny how quickly karma can work sometimes.

Gen's story is a dramatic illustration of how tithing can work. Tithing can also be classed as doing something for somebody for no good reason.

Tithing has much more power if you don't tell anyone, too. Keep your good deeds to yourself. Notice how some people tell everyone? I know a chap called Gary and he's forever telling anyone within earshot how he has a heart of gold and how if any time any of them need a favour he's there for them. At first we all thought what a lovely man, but after a while some friends decided to take him at his word so one by one they asked him a little favour. Maybe a lift a short distance, or could he pick up a pint of milk on his way over. Gary worked for a clothing company and told everyone how they had surplus jumpers: 'Any colour you like – I can get it for you,' he boasted. He never came up with the goods. It was quite amusing watching him say, 'I'd love to, but...' His dream was to become a policeman and every year he failed the tests. I wonder if he had tithed, perhaps things would have turned out differently for him.

Tithing can take many forms. If you follow my suggestions you will start to attract wealth and good luck and, as you do so, the next step is very important: it is then time to give others a helping hand. This sustains and retains your wealth and success and brings up people behind you.

Recently I spoke to an ageing Hollywood actress. She is still working even though she is in her eighties, but at times she struggles and finds it hard to keep up and forgets her lines. The younger actresses adore her but instead of giving them some encouragement she is threatened by them and is rude and critical about them behind their backs.

On the other hand a jazz singer, Salena Jones, who is

acknowledged as one of the greatest singers performing in the world today, recently told me, 'If I see a little girl who may have something in her, some talent, I give her a helping hand. I have been in the business many years and so it's time for me to give something back.' Guess which of the ladies, the Hollywood actress or the jazz singer, looks amazing and vibrant for her age and sleeps well at night? Remember, as you do well, give someone a leg-up and the universe will repay you for your kindness.

> 'You can't help poor people by being one of them'
>
> Abraham Lincoln

Tithing is not just about money. Sometimes it is a kind word or encouragement. I used to pop into a nearby coffee shop in my local supermarket for a break from work. On one particular day a young man walked into the café immaculately dressed. I presumed he'd come for an interview. The manager walked out, looked the young man up and down with a sneer and without shaking his hand or saying hello he said abruptly, 'I will work you very hard, I will pay you very little money and don't expect any thanks.' The young man looked at his feet. The manager continued puffing out his chest boasting about how awful he was to work for and how little reward he gave.

I left and as I drove off I saw the young man walk out of the store. I wound down my window and said, 'Don't take that job, you can do better.' He looked quite startled and said, 'Excuse me?' I repeated what I said then added, 'You are smart, on time and bright. You can do better than work for an awful man like that.' The young man's face broke into the biggest grin I have ever seen and he said, 'Thank you, thank you very much.'

Giving someone some positive feedback or a compliment creates a positive vibration that will echo back to you over and over again.

Chakra Blocks and Abundance

Cosmic Energy needs to flow. Unfortunately, many people are their own worst enemies because they unknowingly block that flow. Every block can be found in your body. Your chakras spin smoothly when flowing well with Cosmic Energy (Cosmic Energy acts as a type of lubricant like oiling the chain on your bike). When you have blocks, your chakras will become slow and sluggish.

The blocks can come from past life or childhood beliefs and experiences, from our fears, disappointments and lack of confidence. By clearing any energy blocks within your chakras you will not only be allowing wealth to flow your way, but you will also retain that wealth instead of living on a financial rollercoaster.

Our bodies reflect back to us our inner beliefs. Often, vital clues are hidden in the charkas, and it's important to explore these blocks because when you know what they are you can clear them.

Unfortunately, sometimes these blocks are so ingrained within you, so entrenched, that they are hard to identify. But look within: the clues are there, and by studying the chakras you will discover where your financial blocks lie. In the following pages you will also learn how to use your Etheric Energy to clear away any debris, get your energy flowing – and reach your full potential.

If you are not receiving wealth then this will be reflected somewhere in your body. Luckily I know exactly how to find the blocks and it's easy to clear them away. Here's how it works.

Check your Chakras

There are seven chakras in the body.

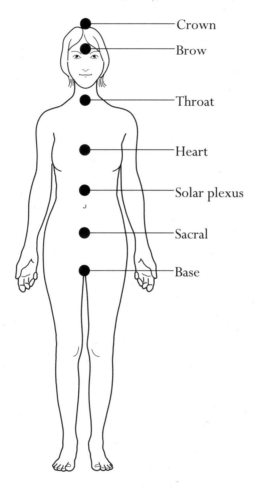

Crown
Brow
Throat
Heart
Solar plexus
Sacral
Base

Each chakra relates to a different part of our lives.

The **base** chakra relates to how grounded we are, how balanced.

The **sacral** chakra represents our sexuality.

The **solar plexus** chakra represents the seat of our emotions.

The **heart** chakra is the energy point that relates to love.

The **throat** chakra is related to how we express ourselves.
The **brow** chakra deals with intuition, study and thinking.
The **crown** chakra connects us to the universe, to Cosmic Energy, and to our higher selves. It brings wisdom.

There are a number of ways you can check your chakra points.

◆ Hold your dominant hand in front of each chakra and feel the temperature change from point to point. A cold point is a sure sign this chakra needs work, while a warm, soft feeling shows this energy point is healthy.

◆ Work with a Tibetan singing bowl. I find this a really good method. You can do this with a friend and check over each other or you can use it on yourself. Simply hold the Tibetan bowl in front of each chakra and as you tap the bowl, notice the clarity, speed and tone of the ring. A dull tone is telling you that the point is also dull and sluggish. A clear, high tone tells you the chakra is running true to form. A cheap-sounding noise, as if the bowl is made from something low quality, tells you this is an important point to clear.

◆ Use a pendulum to dowse the chakras. Hold a pendulum in one hand over the chakra and note how it spins. If it spins clockwise, this indicates a healthy energy flow. Anticlockwise indicates an imbalance.

Get together with a friend or two and try several of the methods and see which you prefer – or use all three to build a strong picture of what is happening with your energy points.

Dull or Slow Energy Points

If while you are checking your chakras you pick up that any particular ones are dull or slow this is what it means:

◆ Base chakra: if you find it hard to get motivated and get going, or hard to stay grounded, this point will be slow. Get this area moving and you will soon have your nose to the grindstone, making steady progress.

◆ Sacral chakra: often people have a feeling of being disadvantaged in some way, for example, such as their sex, religion, age or background, and so expect to fail. Balancing this area brings the confidence to overcome such beliefs.

◆ Solar plexus: this is the seat of emotion where our old beliefs from childhood and past lives reside. If you have been brought up to believe you are not meant to have money, or been given any negative beliefs, this area will need a boost.

Top Tip

Balance in the solar plexus is so important. If you're having problems with creating or retaining wealth, pay special attention to checking out this chakra. It governs emotions, so any 'fear' issues you have around money will be stored as blocked energy in this chakra. By clearing and boosting your energy and realigning this chakra you will be able to step into the vibration of abundance. You will soon notice how opportunities come to you, how doors open and how you generally feel much more positive about your situation – all of which will enable you to move forward into a better space.

◆ Heart chakra: this relates to how you feel about yourself. If you don't believe you deserve abundance, this area will be slow. Putting love into what you do, putting your heart and soul into your work and, ideally, making a living out of your hobby, will help to energise this area.

◆ Throat chakra: this relates to how you express yourself and say what you need to say.

◆ Brow chakra: this relates to the intellect, the need to be mentally stimulated. Boredom will block this area, plus you could over-analyse and convince yourself that money and spirituality don't mix.

◆ Crown chakra: do something to make the world a better place. You are happiest in a job or career that allows you to express your spiritual beliefs in some way, however small. Think artist, writer, priest, healer or counsellor, for example. It is vital that this chakra is spinning beautifully. By allowing this energy point to spin you will find your higher purpose, you will attain abundance and make the world a better place. If this charka is blocked you simply will not be able to stick to an average, mundane job.

So, you know how to check you chakras and identify which ones may be dull, sluggish or slow. Now I'm going to teach you how to energise your slow chakras.

How to Energise Your Chakras

In my first book, *Instant Intuition,* I taught you how to make an energy ball by placing your hands together and channelling your own Etheric Energy. It's amazing – you can easily feel the energy build up. It bounces, almost like having a sponge in your hand. Here is the exercise; it's very easy to do.

The Energy Ball

This exercise will help you sense your energy field. It's subtle, but once you get the hang of it you will become aware of your entire energy field and just what you can do with it.

◆ Hold your hands out in front of you, palms facing each other and about 25cm (10in) apart. Slowly move your palms towards each other. At some point you will feel a slight ball of energy, almost like a bubble. Keep moving your hands, push them slowly towards each other but don't let them touch. Feel the energy and play with it. Feel your hands bounce on and off it. Cup your hands and feel the ball build up energy.

◆ Now rub your hands together briskly for at least five seconds and again bounce your hands towards each other. The energy will be stronger now and you may well feel as if it is trying to push your hands apart. Move your hands backwards and forwards and feel the invisible sponge bouncing between your hands. This is your Etheric Energy.

The Bank of the Universe

I have a cheque on my website www.annejirsch.com that you can print off and write in the amount you want. It is from the great universal bank and it has limitless funds.

The Make-It-Happen Energy Ball

Use the Energy Ball exercise to build up the energy in your hands, then use a powerful telepathic technique to give it life and vibrancy.

◆ Build a very definite image in your mind of what you want. Take as long as you need to make a bright, clear and strong image, at the same time building the energy in your make-it-happen energy ball.

◆ Hold your hands close together and keep building up the energy. Feel and visualise the ball. Keep bouncing your hands together. Now fire the image into the ball – actually imagine your image flying from your mind and into the ball.

◆ Now keep building the same image in your mind and keep firing it into the energy ball.

   Remember to be very specific with your image. If you want a car, What colour is it? What is the upholstery like? Imagine sitting in it, driving it; notice the shine on the bonnet – even the smell. Why not actually go to a showroom and sit in one and take a photograph of the make, model and colour you want?

   If it is money you want, imagine the amount – imagine a pile of money. Fire this image into the energy ball. Imagine your bank statement with an amount on it. Again, be specific.

◆ Now allow your breathing to deepen and breathe into the energy ball. This is your vital life force and by breathing into the energy ball you are breathing life into it. As you breathe into the ball, put emotion into it. Feel how you would feel if you had what you wanted. What difference would it make to your life? How would it make you feel? Calm? Excited? Glowing?

◆ Do this technique once a day for seven days. Then, after one week, take your ball and with two hands throw it high into the air – physically do this, throwing your hands into the air with a great sweeping motion. Feel your energy ball fly off up into the sky and into the universe. This is a fantastic way to use energy and to get your request out there.

Know that your make-it-happen energy ball is out there and your request is being dealt with by the universe. Putting your own energy and life force into the request gives it power.

....

Now you are set up to receive and manifest abundance, let's look at work and career and your ideal way of making that fortune. Remember, the universe helps those who help themselves.

CHAPTER 5
Cosmic Energy at Work

You spend most of your waking life at work. When it drags you down or doesn't fulfil you, it makes you feel miserable. You lose confidence and feel you are wasting your life. This negative emotion rebounds on all areas: health, wellbeing and relationships. Work can break up marriages, give people ulcers, even heart attacks and, in extreme cases where the stress has become unbearable, lead to suicide. Yet work can be the one of the most important areas of your life, giving you a sense of purpose, comradeship and self-esteem, as well as putting food on your table and a roof over your head. Get the work part of your life right and you will be taking a large step towards aligning your energy with the Cosmic Energy surrounding you.

In this chapter you will learn how Cosmic Energy relates to your working life on a personal level (with people) and on a material level (with objects and the space in the workplace). I am going to show you how to align yourself with the universal energy so that Cosmic Energy can flow through you. As a result, you will feel more calm, centred and content. Work can be a very stressful experience but if you know how to tap into and use the tools of Cosmic Energy, you can reduce anxiety and pressure and be more successful.

On a wider level regarding work, once you are using the

power of Cosmic Energy you will create the right circumstances to find your ideal job and life will become less of a
struggle because you will feel more fulfilled. Once your vibration aligns with the universal force and you are working with
Cosmic Energy, you will find that the right job with the right
company, or the right opportunities to start your own venture
will appear. Interviews will go well, you will excel and do a
great job, meet great bosses and colleagues; and create a flow of
opportunities.

In this chapter I will teach you how to:

1. Find your vocation

2. Secure your dream job

3. Achieve success at work

4. Manage a productive and happy team

5. Work with difficult colleagues

6. Give your business the edge

7. Boost your abilities

8. Create sacred space at work

Just imagine if everyone loved their work and was using their
talents, the world would be a much happier place. Just imagine
working in a place that you love. I promise you I cannot wait to
get to my office; it's in a beautiful village in Berkshire and on
the river. I can sit by the Thames and focus and think. It is my
perfect space. I know I will not be here for ever (I have looked
into my future using Future Life Progression, the subject of my
previous book) but for now it is perfect for me. But it hasn't
always been this way.

My first job was as an office junior in a plastics company on a Slough trading estate. I was 16 and felt I had to stay because they were sending me to college one day a week. I couldn't see any other options – other offices were much the same and these people were training me. Then I met an old friend who was working as a temp. She was earning twice as much, had fewer qualifications and she loved going to a different company every week. I handed in my notice and joined her agency. It taught me that there are always other options and we need to find them. As Thomas Edison said, 'There is always a better way.' From getting the right job, to dealing with difficult colleagues and bosses to becoming a success – Cosmic Energy holds the key.

By doing something you love you will create a cosmic flow. The same happens when you have a positive attitude. All work (and business) has its difficulties, but it's your attitude that will make the difference to the final outcome. Study positive people, they're always thinking about how they can make things happen. If they meet an obstacle, they almost light up at the challenge. If you listen to Richard Branson, you can see he has this 'can do' attitude. People tend to think he has the Midas touch and everything he touches turns to gold, listening to him you would think it all dropped into his lap! Yet throughout his career Branson has faced major challenges, but you don't hear him complaining. He focuses on the positive, creating a cosmic flow of energy that makes him luckier and more successful.

If you hate your job, you may have been pushed into the wrong vocation, perhaps into a family business, or pressed to achieve another ambition on behalf of a parent. You might feel you have to stay in a job you hate to provide for your family. But imagine this: imagine going to a doctor who hates his work. Will he or she be a good doctor? Will you feel comfortable with him or her? You know the answer. If you feel negative about your work then change your work – or your attitude.

I'm now going to show you how you can use Cosmic Energy to find your true vocation.

How to Find Your Vocation

Find your perfect career and the best possible place to work and you will be rushing to get to work, excited about what the day holds and be doing something worthwhile to make the world a better place.

'Numbers are the first thing of all nature,' said Pythagoras. I used to be extremely sceptical about numerology but at the insistence of Greta, one of my mentors, I tried it out and discovered my Life Path, which represents what you are destined to do in this lifetime or indicates a task you have to fulfil. My Life Path is nine, which means the number of the traveller and communication. I had to admit that was true, and so I set out to test the theory. I decided that my theatrical and arty friends would have a predominance of the number three – number threes have to express themselves through writing, speaking or any form of creativity. My caring healer friends would be number twos, as they often help others in some kind of service, and so forth. As I tested the theory, I found it uncannily accurate. The people whose life path didn't match their vocation were often lost souls wishing they had followed a different road – the one outlined in their Life Path! In short, look at your Life Path as the spiritual lessons you have been sent here to experience, the destiny you are to face.

Socrates, Plato, Einstein, in fact most of the greatest thinkers, philosophers and mathematicians believed that numbers followed an intricate universal law answering all questions from the big bang to the fate of a newly born child.

I use numerology with all my clients and they are often aston-ished by how much information can be gleaned just from their name and date of birth. Here's how to find your own Life Path using your date of birth.

Find Your Life Path With Numerology

◆ To find your Life Path number, simply write down your date of birth in full.

For example: 12th February 1962 will read 12.02.1962.

Now, add all the numbers together: 12 + 2 + 1 + 9 + 6 + 2 = 32. This will give you a two-digit number, which needs to be further reduced until you reach a single digit (unless your number is 11 or 22), so add those two together. In our example we need to add 3 + 2 = 5, showing that this person's Life Path is five.

Numerologically, your Life Path is your most significant number because it reveals your destiny and what your life path should be, and it never changes.

Working through the example above, work out your own Life Path number. What number are you? Read on to find out what your number reveals about you.

What Your Life Path Number Means

NUMBER ONE: The pioneer. To gain confidence and give strength and leadership to others.

NUMBER TWO: To teach and heal. To understand others and through doing so understand yourself.

NUMBER THREE: Self-expression. To develop your creativity. To heal through the arts, love and spiritual healing.

NUMBER FOUR: To organise and build for the future, for yourself and for others.

NUMBER FIVE: To give energy and life. To help others accept challenge and change. To use energy wisely.

NUMBER SIX: To open your third eye. To investigate and probe the unknown. To study the mind and human behaviour.

NUMBER SEVEN: To integrate the spiritual and material and set an example to others. To develop your intuition to its highest level.

NUMBER EIGHT: To find balance with money. To learn to feel comfortable in a material world and use money wisely for the good of yourself and others.

NUMBER NINE: Wisdom and travel. To travel, gain knowledge and pass on that knowledge for the good of mankind.

Master Numbers

Master vibrations are 11 and 22 and anyone with these numbers has spiritual insight and is often ahead of their time. Their minds are intuitive and tuned in to higher forces.

NUMBER ELEVEN: To be a visionary and messenger, searchers and seekers of the truth.

NUMBER TWENTY-TWO: An idealist who can lead others and build a better world.

Numbers can also really help with assessing how suitable a candidate is for a particular job. I occasionally help companies when recruiting staff because numerology can illustrate the qualities an individual possesses. Handwriting can be changed, psychological tests can be faked, but your date of birth and your name stays the same (unless you go to the trouble of changing official documents). Once a company is down to the final few applicants, I am brought in to build an overall picture showing the strengths and weaknesses of each individual. So far the results have been amazing – and here is just one example.

Sometimes numerology can tell what is left out of a CV. I recently helped a company decide between two candidates. Both had very strong CVs – their credentials were both excellent but the role called for someone who could deal with the unexpected and keep their head in a crisis. I had a feeling one of the applicants had an exciting hobby. In the final interview, they uncovered the fact he took part in extreme sports showing daring, concentration and great strategy. He had the number 11; a master number, showing that he was a visionary which is of great benefit in business as it means he would come up with fresh ideas and solutions to problems. He got the job.

As we have seen, your Life Path is what you are here to do this time around, in this lifetime: you have a task to fulfil or achieve.

I'm now going to teach you how to use numerology to find the area of work that would bring you success and fulfilment, using just your name. I call it your Soul Path because it maps out your strengths and weaknesses and gives more insight into the challenges you may face. You may even have a strong link between your Life Path and Soul Path. Maybe your Life Path is to be a nurse, but your Soul Path is to serve others. If you do past life regression (in which a therapist takes you back in time using hypnosis techniques) you may well find that you have been some type of healer throughout each lifetime as you learn the lessons of your Soul Path.

Finding Your Soul Path With Numerology

Each letter of your name relates to a number. Write out your first name, spreading out the letters, and underneath using the table below write the corresponding number for each letter.

1	2	3	4	5	6	7	8	9
A	B	C	D	E	F	G	H	I
J	K	L	M	N	O	P	Q	R
S	T	U	V	W	X	Y	Z	

Next, as before, add all the digits together until you have a single number (or leave them at 11 or 22 if you are a master number).
e.g. S U S A N J O N E S

1 3 1 1 5 1 6 5 5 1
11 + 18 = 29
2 + 9 = 11

As you can see Susan's name number adds up to 11 which means she has a master number and has the skills to be a writer, an artist, a researcher or a politician, for example; someone who has a vision to make the world a better place. If she didn't want to take on the challenge of a master number, she could consciously take a step back and reduce her name to a two and go into teaching, nursing and dealing with the public.

Also, when having a look at your numerology chart it's wise to take note of a predominance of other numbers. Look at Susan's example – she has several number ones, which give her leadership potential. So if I saw her and she was in the running for a managerial role I would say she had the qualities to take on the challenge. If I saw her numerology chart during recruitment for a junior post, I would point out that she had these strengths and suggest that human resources keep her in mind for promotion in the future. The number five influence is what makes her managerial material, as the vibration of this number gives her the ability to adapt and make decisions.

As a guideline, these are the occupations that best suit each Soul Path.

Soul Path Occupations

NUMBER ONE: Born leader. Manager, decision-maker, organiser, supervisor, executive, promoter, pioneer.

NUMBER TWO: Sensitive and compassionate. Teacher, nurse, healing arts, anything working with or helping the public.

NUMBER THREE: Self-expression. Ability with words: writers, actor, poet, artist, teacher, salesperson, councillor, adviser; also musician, healer, designer.

NUMBER FOUR: Practical. Accountant, bookkeeper, manager, mechanic, builder, computer operator; the backbone of a company.

NUMBER FIVE: Challenge and change. A need to be on the move and making decisions. Driver, company representative, entrepreneur, gardener, company proprietor.

NUMBER SIX: Creative, with strong beliefs of fairness. Social worker, politician, the arts, astrologer, palmist, councillor, caterer, interior designer, charity worker.

NUMBER SEVEN: Psychic and thinker; a need to learn. Clairvoyant, lawyer, doctor, computer programmer, psychiatrist, psychologist, psychic arts.

NUMBER EIGHT: High ambition. Prepared to work their way up in chosen field. Businessperson, accountant, executive, lawyer, diplomat, stockbroker, politician, bank manager.

NUMBER NINE: Travel and wisdom. Working for the good of mankind, a sower of seeds. Cabin crew, pilot, charity worker, politician, alternative health practitioner.

NUMBER ELEVEN: Mental creativity. Writer, politician, artist, researcher.

NUMBER TWENTY-TWO: The power to create change in the world. Leader, business-builder, anthropologist.

Einstein believed that each number vibrates to its own frequency and has a power and energy of its own – which I also believe. Each number has a gift if we can learn to listen to its message. I would like you to work out your Life Path and Soul numbers and write down the information and your thoughts in your Cosmic Journal. If you are feeling lost or alone, reread the descriptions of your Life Path and Soul Paths – it will help to give you strength and focus during difficult times.

How to Secure Your Dream Job

In Chapter 2 I introduced you to Etheric Energy (see page 34). Now you are going to learn how to use EET – Etheric Energy Technique – to tap into a prospective employer, boss or inter-viewee. This technique is easy to follow.

Prepare for your interview with EET

Just imagine being able to get inside information on the company you are applying for a job with, finding out what they are like to work for and what they are looking for in a candi-date. This is so simple to do, and once you have mastered it you can use it to gain insight about meetings, awkward situations – and in all areas of your life.

Don't worry if you have never been to the company's prem-ises and do not know what the building or interviewer looks like. You can just focus on the name of the company or the person who will be interviewing you shown on the letter inviting you for the interview.

I call the EET I am about to teach you the Rainbow River because you visualise Etheric Energy as a strong-flowing, coloured river. (To remind yourself of the basic EET before you begin, see pages 34–5.)

The Rainbow River

◆ Begin with the opening up technique on page 23.

◆ First, focus your energy on the name of the person, or the company, so you can tune in and allow your energy to flow to them. Notice what you feel and any impressions you have. Imagine your energy flowing in through the door and to the person you wish to connect with and want to impress.

◆ Feel your energy flowing towards them like a strong river. Now allow your Etheric Energy to gently rest on their shoulders. Notice what impressions, thoughts and feelings come to you. In your mind ask, 'What do you want? What are you looking for?' Find out all you need to know, as this information will help you to prepare for your interview and give you the edge over other candidates. Spend a few moments tuning in to them. Don't censor what comes into your mind.

◆ Then reclaim your Etheric Energy, imagining the river rushing back to you, but importantly leave a little of your energy in the office or workspace or with the person. You could imagine the Etheric Energy you leave behind as a thin layer of water covering the floor, not stagnant but clear and sparkling.

◆ Carry out the closing down technique on page 24 to finish.

If you want to make this technique even stronger, you can give your Etheric Energy a colour, so you will be visualising coloured water rushing into the building. Think of your energy as a coloured river. As you learnt in Chapter 2, every shade in the spectrum has a particular quality. So if you visualise leaving your coloured Etheric Energy in the interview room, when you meet your interviewer they will attach this quality to you. Infuse your aura with this colour before you actually arrive for your interview. Simply imagine your chosen colour flowing through your aura, pulsating out of you from every pore.

To find the right colour for the job you have applied for, have a look at the following suggestions. Through trial and error I have discovered these work particular well in interviews:

◆ High-profile job such as chairman of the board: infuse your aura with gold.

◆ Jobs with authority: if you are chasing a job in which you need to be respected, such as head of a department or in charge of staff, then silver is perfect.

◆ Dynamic roles: flow some red through your aura.

◆ Communication skills such as in selling or buying or speaking/communicating to the public in some way: yellow is the colour you need.

◆ High-level negotiator: blue is the right colour for you.

◆ Accountancy, or anything to do with budgets and finance: green, because it's the colour of money, and by putting green around you the books will balance and profits will flow. Using green will boost your talents in this area and make them shine.

◆ Creative roles, maybe a graphic designer, window dresser, architect: yellow, similar to communication, but also visualise indigo for inspiration.

If the job you have applied for is not listed, don't worry – all you need to do to find the colour to use with your own EET is to just imagine a rainbow full of different shades. In your mind start with red, then move to orange, yellow, green, blue, indigo and violet. Whichever colour feels right for the job you are applying for is the one to pick. Trust your intuition.

Building the Energy on Interview Day

On the day of your interview, take time to build your energy. This is so simple and can be used without anyone knowing that your Etheric Energy will be doing its job. You can do this anywhere, even in a bustling coffee shop.

Sit and focus on what you want to achieve. Take time to know exactly what you want to gain from this meeting or interview. Do not just say to yourself, 'I want the job.' What package do you want? What hours? Pay? How do you want your colleagues to be? Do you want to hit the floor running or ease in gradually? Focus on what you want.

Now think about all the things that have gone well in your life, the successes and achievements. Think about what exams you have passed, focus on how you felt when you passed your driving test or learnt to swim. Focus on when work has gone exceptionally well. Notice where you feel this in your body. Now allow this feeling to flow right through you and, as you do so, amplify it and make it stronger.

Now allow the feeling to extend beyond you so that it flows through your aura. Now, as described before (see page 157), send more of your EE ahead of you. Infuse it with the colours that represent the qualities you want to impress them with at the meeting. Think about the times you have felt confident and all the things that have gone well.

Using Etheric Energy at Your Interview

As you enter the room for your interview fill it with your aura. Allow your aura to really shine brightly, infused with the colours you have chosen. Put vibrancy and good feelings into your energy, then let go. You can concentrate on your interview knowing you have the edge over the other candidates.

I have many clients in show business and I teach them how to use their EE during auditions, which when you think about it are a special kind of interview. At times there are dozens, even hundreds, of people all auditioning for the same role – so you need the edge. If you are auditioning, you want to stand out and make the casting director notice you. As you are waiting for your audition, fill the room with your energy – make sure you flow some gold through your energy field to enhance your charisma. Now send it to the casting director/s in the room. During the audition, you can use your EE to actually touch the casting director. Imagine your brilliant, bright, white etheric energy reaching out of your body and touching the casting director. As you leave, give them a big smile and be sure to leave a little of your energy behind in the room. Even when the next candidate arrives they will still be thinking about you and what you have to offer.

After trying the technique, jobbing actress Leslie told me recently, 'Since I have used this I have been shortlisted three times for bigger roles and twice been given a key role. Before, I had been in the acting wilderness for four years and was on the point of giving up. Now they always say the same thing: "I don't know what it is but you have something."'

Case Study

A client, Sharon, was going for a job as a manager in a high-profile events company specialising in sporting events. She would be called upon to travel at a moment's notice and juggle several events at one time, often in the public eye. Sharon really wanted the job and as she had been made redundant and was struggling financially, she was desperate to land this role.

Sharon told me, 'As I sat on the train travelling to my interview I focused on what I wanted and all the things that had gone well in the past to create some positive energy around me. My last job had ended badly, but I refused to let that creep in.

'I then focused on flowing some red through my aura. I saw it glowing all around me. I chose red because I knew this role called for someone with plenty of energy. As I stepped into the room and shook hands with the interviewer, I visualised myself pulsating with this shade. I got the job.'

Use EET to Find the Right Candidates for the Job
You can also use Etheric Energy at interviews if *you* are the interviewer.

Bruce runs a large organisation that he has built up from scratch. He is hands-on and always likes to know who works for him and what is going on. He conducts every interview himself. I taught Bruce to use his EE while interviewing prospective employees. Bruce told me, 'When I interview someone now, I use my Etheric Energy and gently touch them on the shoulder with this energy. As I do so, words come into my mind.' He told that recently he had interviewed a girl and used his usual Etheric Energy Technique, as he did so the words 'stop gap' came into his mind.

'After the interview I looked over her CV closely and I could see that she had worked at a much higher level in the past but had not done so well in recent years. It made sense she would see this role as a stop gap until she got something at a higher level.'

Bruce wanted someone who would be there for a long time. He told me, 'I would be investing a lot of time and effort into whoever took this role. It was a new phase for my company. The last thing I needed was someone who would be off as soon as something else came along.' Later he interviewed a young man and he said, 'As my Etheric touched his shoulder the words, "I would love this job" came to me. I could feel he was a little bit shy but I knew I could bring him out. I gave it to him on the spot and his face broke into the biggest grin. I knew I had my apprentice. He is still with me three years later and has had two big promotions. He is a great lad and a valued member of staff.'

How to Achieve Success at Work

I teach Etheric techniques in the workplace more than any of my other techniques – it is both subtle and effective. While using your Etheric Energy you will be aware, for example, when your boss is a bit down in the dumps, needs back-up or perhaps needs to be left alone. You will be able to anticipate situations more accurately and you will be more in tune with events.

Think back – have you ever worked with someone with whom you had an amazing connection? You probably could anticipate each other's ideas and needs. You can have that connection again using Cosmic Energy, which will strengthen your link with your boss over and above your colleagues. You can also use it to stand out and be noticed; you can use it to create (to put out energetically) whatever impression you need to at a given time. I'm about to teach you how to do all of these things.

Communicate Openly With Your Boss

Joan had been a client of mine for many years. She is a strong and capable person, so I was surprised when she told me she felt badly treated at work and found it impossible to talk to her boss. She told me, 'I just can't ask him for a pay rise or discuss the work. He is so unapproachable. I steel myself to talk to him but find myself babbling on while he looks sternly at me over his glasses.' Joan went on to say his response was either that he would speak to her later, which he never did, or told her to speak to his secretary, who informed her that there was nothing she could do. Joan added, 'I'm left feeling humiliated and annoyed with myself for being so pathetic.'

I taught Joan how to connect with her boss on an astral level and the results for her were incredible. Joan told me, 'Talking to him on the astral level meant I didn't have to be overly polite, it was one to one and I felt in control. The funny thing is I could feel him squirming and trying to slip away.'

Joan knew she had a right to be heard and this way worked perfectly for her. She told him how she felt about talking to him, how she felt overworked and underpaid. Joan used her Etheric Energy to tap into him and immediately knew that he was actually very nervous himself. His sternness was a cover-up for his inability to communicate and deal with people.

The next day he didn't come into work, which was unheard

of. The following day, an extraordinary thing happened. He walked into the room, looked at Joan slightly alarmed and then went into his office without a word. One week later he gave everyone a pay rise. The funny thing was, he began to talk to Joan. He would ask her how she was and how her job was going. Joan told me, 'He became much chattier, a much better boss and a nicer person.'

I'm now going to show you how you can astral-travel from the comfort of your armchair, or lying down on your bed.

....

How to Connect on the Astral Plane with Etheric Energy

Do this exercise when you have plenty of time and you are not liable to have people popping in or have something urgent to do. Find yourself a comfy place to relax, lower the lights, close your eyes and relax.

♦ Begin with the opening up technique on page 23.

♦ Allow your breathing to soften. Focus on your breath, breathing in through your nose and out through your mouth softly and gently. Allow your body to feel light and floaty as you let go of your day-to-day cares and worries. Feel yourself moving beyond the mundane and into your more spiritual self.

♦ Become aware of the inner energy that is you, the essence that is the real you – locate it. Your subconscious mind knows exactly where it is; allow your instincts to guide you. Where are you are drawn? Keep gently breathing in through your nose and out through your mouth and sense where your true essence is. Some people feel it is around their heart or forehead or their crown. Don't worry where it is – even if it is in your big toe, just allow yourself to be guided by your instincts.

◆ Focus on that Etheric Energy, connect with it and enjoy the feeling of being aware of the true you, the immortal, eternal you, your life force. Send your thoughts to above your head. Focus on your Etheric Energy rising upwards – keep gently moving it upwards and upwards and as it rises upwards feel it becoming lighter and lighter, rising up and out of your body until you feel yourself floating just above your own head. Stay there for a while just floating and being aware of being suspended in space – just your essence. Enjoy feeling free.

Remember that your thoughts are a big influence on your astral journey, so think very clearly about where you want to be, who you want to talk to and what you want to say to them.

◆ Now focus on travelling to the specified person. Don't worry about where they are or what they are doing – simply focus all your intent on connecting with them. Be aware of the person and feel yourself in front of their Etheric Energy.

◆ Connect with their Etheric Energy. Take a moment to notice how they are feeling. You can use your Etheric Energy to feel their energy. Now talk to their energy, and as you connect more of it will arrive. Take as long as you wish to connect with their energy and to tell them what you need to say. Allow time to feel their response. Whatever you feel or think is their true response and not what they say in their waking

166 The Power of Manifesting

time. Very often words will pop into your head or you may get a strong feeling or image. Accept whatever comes to you.

◆ When you are ready, simply think the words, 'Back to body' and you will immediately reconnect with your earthly self but now with the knowledge you need.

◆ Carry out the closing down technique on page 24 to finish.

....

By astral travelling you actually walk into the place and situation. It is so much more than just gaining an image, or a thought or feeling. When you astral travel and use your Etheric Energy you're actually stepping into it, so you engage all your senses. You can feel, see and even hear. You can use astral travel to make your work life easier, to gain a little inside information or to find out what someone is thinking or doing. Why not try out the following:

◆ Astral travel to your boss. Find out what their greatest pressure is and find a way to help them with it.

◆ Find out what your colleagues or a competitor are up to.

◆ Use it to discover which person would be your best mentor.

Don't underestimate the power of this technique and don't censor the information you receive, go with your flow. Gilly, a client with a stressful job, uses this technique to stay one step ahead of her demanding boss.

Case Study

Gilly, who works in corporate banking, told me, 'My field is very competitive. At times my senior manager in my last post asked odd questions to provoke a response and sometimes it was very difficult to know what response he wanted. This management technique is applied throughout the company, so if you want to get on you have to know how to play the game and what your boss is thinking.

'Once I learnt the astral travel method, I had a good idea of what questions he was going to ask – and what response he was looking for to see how I was performing. Now I have a fantastic new high-powered job with the same firm and I'm sure this technique gives me an edge. I'm able to stay one step ahead of my boss and no longer panic when he starts asking questions, "playing the game", because I know what's coming and how to win.'

Top Tips for Astral Travel

◆ A good time is when you are about to sleep or have just woken up. At these times you are already between two places and your energy is already in between states.

◆ You will get better with practice, so start very gradually and with little jaunts.

◆ On rare occasions you may come across something you do not like or are not comfortable with. Just literally say the word 'body' and you will snap straight back. If you are a little nervous then do it during the day in broad daylight, or even outside in the sunshine.

◆ On the astral level things can seem quite odd. You may feel as if you still have your body – some people comment that they are wearing clothes, for example. You also become quite pliable – you can stretch your arms for miles if you wish. You may look older or younger. One wonderful benefit is people in pain enjoy being pain-free.

◆ Start off with simple trips. Don't be too adventurous; by building up your astral travel you earn your astral wings.

◆ The more you focus on where you want to be, the more likely you are to get there. Try focusing on a photograph to help the connection.

How to Manage a Productive and Happy Team

Meetings have often been called 'the biggest waste of time'. I see many people who have endless meetings in which nothing is ever decided and the participants even seem to be working against each other. The same can be said for idea-generating sessions. Yet handled well, with a good productive meeting everyone can get on track, focus and generate brilliant ideas. I have found that some companies are open to experimental and spiritual work while others fall off their chairs in horror at the suggestion.

The companies I have worked with have all reported a tremendous boost in productivity and morale. Most of the exercises I am about to show you are easy to use, whether the company you work for is open-minded or not. You can do them without anyone knowing.

Finding the Negative Team Member

If you have a group that seems to be working against itself, the following exercise will let you know who is a problem and who isn't. It's a dynamic way to study your team.

♦ At the beginning of the meeting focus on your aura and make it bigger and bigger and brighter. Now run some silver through it. This gives you authority over the group without them knowing it.

♦ Now allow your Etheric Energy to grow (see page 34) and let a tiny part touch each person in the room. You will probably want to do this once the discussion has started. Allow your energy to connect with their aura and draw their energy towards you. You will feel a little bit of their energy connect with yours. Take a moment to notice who comes willingly, who resists and who is hard to connect with.

♦ Notice what thoughts and feelings flow to you as you connect with each person. There is probably at least one who says all the right things but when you connect you will find they are not on your side at all – and will probably be working against you with negative comments behind your back.

Now allow their energies to flow to the centre point – this is usually the centre of the meeting table. Allow their energies to blend, noticing if there is any resistance from any of the participants. If so, they are not working well with the others. Has anyone there blended well with the others, who would make a good manager? Could you ask them to take over leading the project? If they are open-minded you can teach them how to enhance their aura and instruct them to send it to the centre of the room. If not, you can simply pull their energy towards you.

....

How to Work With Difficult Colleagues

Okay, so you have checked out your staff. Now I'm going to show you how to work with your negative or unproductive team members.

You are back in the meeting room and have built up your aura using the technique from Chapter 2 (see page 32) – where you see yourself surrounded by a sparkling aura. Now I'm going to teach you how to take this technique one step further using colour. In a moment you will see a list of colours and their various properties, their energies. All you have to do is pick a colour to help you overcome whatever work issue it is you face. Imagine this colour flowing from your aura into your colleagues' auras, swirling around them and engulfing them with its power. Don't forget, the colours you project using this aura technique will enhance your team and help them to move forward in the best possible way. For example, if your team has been arguing or not getting along just send out a lot of white and soft blues. Send a wave of the colour out to everyone and soon you will notice people in the room softening and becoming easier to deal with. If there is any one person who seems to be a rebel or difficult, send them an extra boost of blue.

The Colours

◆ Fresh ideas: If you need your team to generate fresh and exciting ideas, send them yellow to boost the creative flow.

◆ Wake them up: Red will revitalise a team.

◆ To calm things down: Send them blue. This healing colour will help cool down a heated discussion.

◆ My favourite colour to use in meetings is orange. I usually want to stimulate the participant's energy but a lot of red can often be too much – orange is the combination of red to raise their energy and vibrancy and yellow for ideas and communication. Orange will make people feel good and alive and let them forget any petty grievances they may have.

◆ Finish by blending your energy with theirs – now send your energy to all the participants and allow them to mingle. Actually feel your energies blending. This really works well, especially if you are running a special project together.

You can also use your aura to lie low at work or to get noticed, and the great news is no one will know that you are doing it. When you need to keep a low profile, simply focus on your aura and reduce its size and colours. Actually imagine your aura folding in like butterfly wings and becoming fainter and lighter. When the boss is on the warpath this will keep you off his or her radar. Once they have gone, you can unfold your butterfly wings – and switch your aura back on again.

I taught this technique to Pauline, who worked in administration at an engineering company. Several times a week her boss would look for someone to run an errand for him. The problem was that running this errand would make Pauline leave work late and meant a difficult journey home. Plus, she wasn't getting paid any extra cash for working overtime. But by using this technique, her boss began to ask others in the office who lived nearer to the delivery point to run the errand instead.

How to Give Your Business the Edge

Many of my clients who work in sales use EET to discover what their customers need or even what their objections are to closing a deal. Steve told me, 'Sometimes it's hard to find why a customer no longer wants to buy from you. I use EET to tap into them and find out exactly what is going on. Then I can overcome and find a solution or compromise to their objection.'

You can also use EET to infuse your products with energy to ensure they achieve success in the marketplace. Last year some friends of mine mentioned that they were becoming 'addicted' to food from a certain restaurant. Each day they would pop down for their lunch and somehow could never get enough. One day, one of the group, Anna, jokingly asked the chef if he had a magic ingredient to make the food so moreish. He told her, 'I put a little of my special love and energy into each meal before it leaves. It is like blessing the food.' This is a great example of how positive energy can draw you to a place, person or location. In this case, the chef was using his own EE to give the food sparkle and achieve business success.

How to Boost Your Abilities

Often we need a boost of confidence, motivation or talent and an ability cloak can quickly bring you the skill, the ability, you want and need. You can keep it with you for as long as you wish. I love ability cloaks because they do what they say – they cloak you with the ability of your choice. They can give you an air of authority or motivation, and manifest any quality you wish.

Say you want to feel more confident. Just think of the time you felt the most confident; maybe it was passing your driving test, getting married, or being given a wonderful compliment. Well, this is the feeling you will instantly have while wearing your ability cloak. When you are wearing one you are surrounding yourself with the desired energy, so if you put on a 'confidence ability cloak' you are cloaking yourself with a confidence vibration. What's more, the cloaks are not affected by outside events such as being influenced by what people say or do.

Your Wardrobe of Ability Cloaks

◆ Relax, shut your eyes and see yourself inside a vast cave. I would like you to walk to the other side and notice a huge oak wooden door; put your hand on the handle and the door slides open. Only you can open this door. It leads to your special room. The room is cosy and comfy with rich warm colours, thick carpet and long silk curtains adorning the rich cream walls. Everything in this room is tasteful and luxuriously plush.

◆ You look across the room to a long oval mirror on a stand. There is a large dark oak wardrobe with the words 'ability closet' etched deeply on the door.

◆ Walk over to the wardrobe. Inside is a long line of cloaks; you can immediately see that these are no ordinary cloaks; they have something very special and magical about them.

Each cloak is on its own hanger with a label attached. Each

cloak is a slightly different colour. You reach out to the first cloak and look at the label. On the label is the word 'courage'.

◆ You reach out for the first cloak and put it on. This cloak will give you the courage to do things you would never have dared before. It will give you the courage to stand your ground, the courage to handle situations that would usually daunt you, the courage to take up new things that will enhance your life. Stop for a moment and think about all the times you have wished you'd had more courage.

◆ In the workplace, the cloak you may find the most useful is the one for confidence. Look around. Where is this cloak hanging? You instantly know which cloak is right for you and as you put it on it feels like the cosiest softest cloak ever made – yet you know it's powerful and keeps you safe.

◆ Stand in your confidence cloak and know you have the confidence to step up to the challenge. When you put on this cloak, notice how you stand differently, breathe differently and think differently. As you put on this cloak you will believe in yourself and in your abilities and talents. No matter where you are or what you do, you will feel really good about yourself.

◆ There are many spare ability cloaks in your wardrobe. Whatever ability you want you can have by putting on the cloak.

◆ While you are looking at the cloaks notice there is a pen and spare labels. Write on the label the ability you would like to have and place it on the hanger of the spare cloak. Really think about the ability you would like and how it would affect your life. You can write anything you wish on this label:

determination, creativity, calmness, kindness, sensuality – whatever quality you need right now. As you put on the cloak think in great detail how good your life would be if you had this ability. Feel it, taste it, smell it, hear it and see it.

Spend some time wearing your cloak. When you are finished, hang it back up.

Note: If you like, you can imagine continuing to wear your cloak for as long as you wish. This can be particularly helpful when you have a special situation to deal with.

....

Clients have used the cloak of courage to go for a promotion, ask for a pay rise or put themselves forward for a team leader role. It also works to ward off negative vibrations from others in the workplace and in other situations, or to give them wisdom to make the right move and get a job well done.

Case Study

Simon was made fun of at work and ridiculed. When he came to me for a confidence-boosting session he was a nervous wreck and very unhappy. He told me, 'I'd started my dream job in a high-powered sales office full of energy, ready to build my ideal career. Unfortunately my firm was particularly cliquey, with a bullying ringleader who poked fun at me on a daily basis. I soon found I was regularly the butt of jokes with others joining in.

During the confidence-boosting session, I told Simon about the ability cloaks and how they work. I then instructed Simon to go to his special room and choose the cloak most appropriate for his need. He told me, 'It's a cloak of fortitude.' As he said the words he immediately looked stronger and more resolute.

Two days later Simon called me to say, 'I imagine that I'm wearing the cloak the entire time I'm at work. In fact it goes on as I arrive in the car park. I found myself walking differently. I really feel I have an air of authority now. The funny thing is, the bully went to say something the first day I was wearing it, and then looked away. I am certain he feels intimidated and since then people have been leaving me alone and I feel I am able to shine and get on with my job.'

How to Create Sacred Space at Work

Now, I am going to teach you how to create a sacred space at work. We are stepping out of the realms of the energy you can create to manipulate with your mind the energy that interacts on a material level – the space before your eyes.

I mentioned earlier that after leaving my first job as an office junior I worked as a temp. Every week I would work at a different company, covering staff shortages due to holidays, pregnancy and staffing shortfalls. It was fascinating to find how at some companies I would immediately feel at home yet at others I would experience a feeling of dread the second I walked through the door. Such places would usually have a high staff turnover and high rate of conflicts and tribunals.

In the workplace it is vital to allow chi, the universal energy, to flow positively, creating an almost fresh happy feeling in its wake. If you have areas of stale negative energy you will have problems with staff, colleagues, customers and products. Orders will not be delivered, staff will not stay and it is likely there will be a high rate of absenteeism due to sickness.

So let's get your workspace buzzing and feeling wonderful. Whether you own and run the organisation or simply occupy the corner of a desk; whether the company is huge or just one or two people, or your office is in your home, the following techniques will create a sacred space for you at work. If you work in a busy environment it may be worth staying late or coming in on a Saturday, or some time when no one is about, to carry out some of the techniques such as using sound to clear your space. You might not want to be caught by your boss brandishing a Tibetan singing bowl!

Most work colleagues will not bat an eyelid when you spray your space as most people will presume you are making your area smell good. Little will they know you will be changing the energy.

The Five-point Plan to Create a Sacred Space at Work

STEP ONE: Make the Space Your Own
If you have just started a new job it's the perfect time to clear the space and make it your own. Clear away as much of the previous occupant as you can, especially any personal items they may have left behind such as their plants, pictures, photographs and ornaments. The more personal the item, the more of their energy they have left behind. This is especially vital if you want to make your own mark on the company.

Top Tip

One exception to obliterating the presence of your predecessor is if you have taken over the space of someone exceptional whom you would aspire to be in your working life. In this case, leave their energy there for at least a few weeks for you to absorb, then clear the space as before to create your own energy, your own sacred space.

Have a good clear-out, even if most of the paperwork or tools of the trade will not be changed. Clear out each space and dust and clean with bicarbonate of soda to remove any negativity. Go through each item before you put it back. Spending half a day space-clearing will make a huge difference to your working life. You can do this in a new office, or your existing one. A feather duster is great for breaking up old stale energy and getting that chi flowing.

If there is paperwork from your predecessor that you need to keep, quickly flick through each page to allow clean air to circulate – again, this only need take a few minutes. You can flick through a whole book in a few seconds.

STEP TWO: Creating Flow

Try to have very little on the floor because it blocks the flow of chi. If you are in a cubicle or a very square space, or by a long corridor or walkway, put a sizeable crystal near the entrance to your space as it will draw the positive energy to you. If the energy flows too quickly past you, you will go unnoticed in the workplace and good things, like promotions, will flow straight past you as well.

Throw away anything you do not really need — often in the workspace there are several copies of items like phone books and paperwork. Usually these can be thrown away without anyone really noticing.

STEP THREE: Sweeping Away the Old Energy
Somehow you need to break up the energy to give your space a fresh, vibrant feel, but you cannot always clap or ring bells at your workplace.

If possible, try to stay late or go to work during the weekend when no one is about so when you feel a build-up you can use bells, or clapping. Clapping stirs up stale and stagnant energy. When you clap your hands it creates a sound wave, like any noise, but is a short sharp vibration which gets the energy moving again.

Case Study

Julie, a troubleshooter and management consultant, is also very sensitive to energy. She says, 'I am called into companies that have problems, but before I look at the accounts I feel the energy of the place. Usually the office is full of stagnant energy, which I clear away. I do this by filling each room with bright white light and imagine any debris or dark paths lurking in the corners flying out of the window – being sucked out like a mini tornado. I also bring a small music player with me and play clearing music such as Tibetan monks chanting or soft chill-out music. I tell my clients the music relaxes me. Little do they know I am clearing the stagnant energy for them.'

Julie tells the company to clear away any junk, boxes and items on the floors. She tells them that it creates confusion and is untidy. She says, 'I do not try to explain that I am sorting out the energy as well as working on a practical level. It is enough that I tell them that they need to be tidy and organised and that I get the results.'

STEP FOUR: Finding Your Spot

The next step is to experiment with the placement of furniture; little things make a huge difference like not having your back to a door or window and having room to move. Your instincts will be your perfect guide.

Try placing your chair at different angles or in different places. We all have own power spot – the place that just feels right for you – and once you find yours you will work to a high standard and have heaps of energy.

Have something personal in your space that is symbolic to you. Do not have ten teddy bears, half a dozen photographs and a yucca plant on your desk – just have one select item that represents your own success, maybe a picture of a mountain or a sacred place.

STEP FIVE: Creating Energy

The final step is creating energy. We constantly create energy every time we think, talk, put on music, decide who to call. Imagine relaxing at home. The door bell rings and in front of you is someone you dread visiting. Your energy and the energy in your home will completely change in seconds because that visitor has created energy. You are about to produce positive energy and create and control any mood you desire.

Using the work spray is the most subtle way to create a positive vibration in the workspace and combines a number of powerful tools.

Your Work Spray

You can make your own work spray using selected ingredients from the lists below. You can benefit from a blast of Cosmic Energy, whenever you need it – spray it on work files and even your work shoes before an important meeting. You can also use the spray as a personal spray. You can choose the most relevant crystal for you and place it on your workspace, or energise your drinks by placing the crystal in your glass for a few minutes before drinking.

The Spray Ingredients

Bach Flower Remedies

- Centaury: Promotes self-worth. If you put others first to the detriment of yourself, pick this one.

- Larch: Wonderful for people who lack confidence or do not feel good enough.

- Sweet chestnut: Gives the courage needed to take a completely new direction.

- Star of Bethlehem: If you have suffered a great upset or upheaval such as losing your business, being made redundant or bankrupt or a fear of failure, this helps you overcome negative emotions.

- Holly: If you envy the success of others this remedy will help dissolve the negative emotion of jealousy.

- Gorse: If you are feeling as if there is no hope, or cannot imagine life ever improving, this will nurture positive emotions.

- Chestnut bud: If you keep finding yourself in the same old rut, this is what you need right now; helps to break out of old patterns.

- Wild oat: When you cannot work out your true path, this will give you clarity and help you find your true path.

- Oak: If you confuse activity with achievement this will help you to focus better. I often use this for clients who work incredibly hard but never get anywhere.

- Gentian: When you have had a number of setbacks this will give you the determination to keep going.

Crystals

- Topaz: Helps release your creativity.

- Amethyst: Promotes clarity, clear thinking, and the ability to make better decisions.

- Citrine: Helps make you more powerful.

- Clear quartz: Boosts clear thinking.

- Garnet: Ideal for strength of character, a 'keep-going' attitude.

- Moonstone: When the goals seem so big and out of reach, moonstone helps to break them down into bite-sized pieces.

- Obsidian: Helpful if you tend to procrastinate. This helps you focus on the important things, like keeping accounts.

- Pyrite: Helps you to take an idea and make it more concrete.

- Tiger's eye: Promotes concentration and focus, and brings solid cash.

- Black tourmaline: Clears negative thoughts.

Essential Oils

- Peppermint: For clear intention. Use before a meeting to make sure you are clear in what you say and in knowing what you want to achieve.

- Basil: Also good before a meeting, to give you strength and strong decision-making skills.

- Patchouli: This was used by merchants when they took long journeys to buy and sell their wares. It helped them make clever decisions and gave them an air of richness.

- Fennel: To stop others trying to steal your business or work, and to stop people getting in your way.

- Rose: To make people become drawn to you and your services or business.

- Orange: Makes you optimistic and positive.

- Frankincense: Promotes abundance and wealth.

The workplace is more competitive than ever these days and no one can ever be sure they have a job for life. Using Cosmic

Energy in the form of Etheric Energy Techniques and in work sprays gives you the edge at work, creates the perfect environment for your skills and gives you the information that you need to do a great job and be one step ahead at all times.

When your mind and body are flowing with Cosmic Energy, you are ready to move towards getting your wisdom flowing and in the next chapter we will be looking at your Life Purpose and what you need to learn in order to grow. We will be connecting to a deeper energy that is the eternal you, and discovering how the universe sends us coincidences to help keep us on track.

CHAPTER 6

Find Your Life Purpose

Everyone has a reason for being here, but it's easy to feel lost and it can seem as if you don't know which road to follow. Sometimes you just need to find the next step, the next part of your journey. In this chapter you will discover how to use Cosmic Energy to find your Life Purpose, the reason you are here now on this earth.

If you are wondering what I mean by 'Life Purpose', let me put it this way: how would you like to live your life using your talents to the full, learning what you need to learn and doing what you can to make the world a better place? We all have something to contribute while we are here – this is our Life Purpose. The great thing is that it's usually tied in with our vocation, our work, and linked to what we love doing the most. So if you love flowers you need to be a flower arranger or florist – or maybe grow flowers. If you love animals, then find a way to help and work with them. If you love colour and design, train to be an interior decorator, graphic designer or window dresser. The clues are always around you.

When you are not working and living in line with your Life Purpose, life becomes hard and a constant struggle, and you wonder why you are not moving forward. Once you find your true purpose and you align with Cosmic Energy, everything flows – which is why when you are on the right track suddenly doors open, the right mentors appear and you love every moment of every day. In this chapter I will look at:

1. Blocks

2. Coincidences and Cosmic Energy

3. Universal Clues

4. What is Your Life-purpose Ratio?

5. The Bigger Picture

Cosmic Energy is all around you and each and every tiny cell of your body contains all that you will ever need to know. It's believed that the human body contains between fifty and 100 trillion cells and each cell holds twenty-three pairs of chromosomes that contain your code – your DNA. This is your blueprint.

Now I want to take you forward a giant leap in your thinking. I want to tell you about holograms. If you look at a hologram it contains a complete image and if you cut it in half, each half will contain a complete image. Cut it into four and all four pieces will contain a full image. You can snip off the tiniest piece and it will still contain the full image. Many eminent scientists now think that our reality is created by a hologram (and yes, they came up with these ideas before the film *The Matrix*). The theory is that every cell in your body is a hologram. It contains not only your blueprint but the blueprint of everyone else on the planet plus anyone who has ever lived, who ever will live and all the knowledge in the universe. Does this theory sound far-fetched?

Karl Pribram, a professor of neuropsychology at Stanford University, California, believes that the brain itself is a hologram and whatever images we put into our holographic brain is projected into our world and lives. Pribram's theory explains how the human brain can store so many memories in so little space. It has been estimated that the human brain has the capacity to memorise something in the order of ten billion bits of information during the average human lifetime (or roughly the same amount of information contained in five sets of the *Encyclopedia Britannica*).

Dr Stanislav Grof, Chief of Psychiatric Research at the Maryland Psychiatric Research Center in the US, believes a holographic model can explain such things as archetypal experiences, encounters with the collective unconsciousness and other unusual phenomena experienced during altered states of consciousness. While Dr Fred Alan Wolfe (also known as Dr Quantum) believes holograms explain lucid dreams.

I believe, along with many forward-thinking quantum physicists, that as well as our brain our bodies are also holograms and there are clues everywhere. In Chinese acupuncture the belief is that every organ and bone in the body is connected to acupuncture points. There are over one thousand of these points in the body. But also within the body are points on the feet that correlate to the various organs and by stimulating these points you can stimulate the flow of energy. Reflexologists use these energy points to heal the mind, body and spirit.

Less known is that your ear also contains a similar system. French physician and acupuncturist Paul Nogier discovered that each ear contains a little map of a human body curved like a tiny foetus. At the time Nogier had no idea that the Chinese also used this system and called the map 'little man of the ear'. Nogier's book *Treatise of Auriculotherapy* was published in 1957 and since then Dr Terry Oleson, a psychobiologist at the pain management clinic at the University of California, has discovered that he could accurately diagnose what was happening in a patient's body using the 'little man of the ear' map.

You may not agree with the hologram idea, but it is important to understand that each and every cell of your body tells your story. Everything you need to know is within you – you are connected to the universe, to Cosmic Energy.

At the moment of your conception you were a tiny single cell that became two then four and grew and grew. Each cell had all the information of the universe within it. It is a total hologram.

You were born strong, confident, loved and powerful. You were fearless, uninhibited and unafraid to demand what you wanted. You had no judgement of whether anyone was pretty or ugly or what colour they were, whether they were rich or poor. You loved everyone unconditionally.

You were connected to everything and everything was connected to you. But then, as we saw in Chapter 3 with regard to your love life and relationships, you were given blocks.

Blocks

Blocks can be given to you by your parents, siblings, family, teachers and even friends. They are called blocks because they block your flow through life. The first block was fear: don't touch, it will hurt you, don't run, don't climb the tree. That's not safe, and there is danger everywhere. It's right that you are given some warnings for safety but many of the commands given to you from your parents are passing on their own fears such as, 'Don't stroke that strange dog, it's dirty', when the dog is perfectly clean!

Then bit by bit, you were taught separation: keep away from the people up the road they are different from us, keep away from the poor/rich people, those from another place, the smelly people, the ones who are different from us. Don't play with those kids because they are rough or have odd ways. They will hurt you.

Next came the criticism. You are too fat/thin, too young /too old, you are the wrong colour/shape, you cannot do that. That is not for the likes of you. You are not good at . . . you are not clever enough.

Then you were taught pain. If you love you will be hurt; people will leave you and break your heart. You will feel rejected. Don't try, then you won't get hurt.

Bit by bit the blocks grew and stopped you being all you could be, from achieving your potential, your Life Purpose. The blocks created separation and we separated from others, from ourselves and from the universal flow. Life became harder and harder. When this happens, the universal energy, the Cosmic Energy becomes fragmented and you can no longer flow through life.

As we grow up we are taught many negative blocks that we integrate into our reality, our everyday lives. When I was growing up my aunts used to say to me, 'Have fun before you get married because you won't have any afterwards.'

Another of their favourite sayings was: 'Those that have money keep it among themselves' and, 'If you don't trust anyone you can't go far wrong.'

The following exercise will help you to reconnect with your true universal self, your Cosmic Energy.

....

Removing the Blocks

◆ Find yourself a comfy place to relax and make sure you will not be disturbed because this exercise is important. It will reconnect you to your soul energy, your blueprint, your Life Purpose.

◆ Close you eyes and allow your breathing to deepen. As you do this, become aware of yourself and how you have arrived at where you are today. Keep focusing on your breathing and know that you have travelled through many lifetimes to be where you are right now.

◆ Now imagine you are floating back in time, back through the years, right back through your younger years to your childhood. Back to being a baby – so lovely, so soft. Flow right back to your birth. Be aware of the moment you came into the world. A fresh start, a chance to learn and grow. How does it feel?

◆ Keep flowing back, right back to being in the womb. Feel safe and warm in your incubator inside your mother.

◆ Float back to the very moment you were conceived. The actual moment you came into being. You were just one tiny cell.

◆ Now imagine you have that cell in the palm of your hand. The cell that is the beginning of you. Just know that cell contains all the knowledge of the universe, your DNA, your personal blueprint of who you are, and all that you have ever been. All you have been and all you will ever be. It is all there in the palm of your hand.

◆ Look at that tiny cell and know that this is who you are and who you are to become. Your whole character, your whole personality is in the cell. Know how powerful that cell is.

◆ Feel positive love towards that tiny cell then watch as it splits into two, knowing that your new journey has begun. Your new adventure into your current lifetime, for that is what it is – an adventure. With happiness and joy, with heartbreak, with challenges, some that are met and some that will fail. The life to be lived by you, just like an epic movie. As you go from scene to scene in your lifetime, know that you are the hero of this adventure. From now on you will face each day as a hero on your journey, taking whatever happens in your stride, both good and bad.

◆ Your energy is strong, and has survived lifetime after lifetime. The energy that is you was here before the earth and before even the universe and it will be here after it.

◆ As you focus on that tiny cell hold it, feel its power, know that it contains everything you need to know, this cell is like a crystal ball.

The next part of the exercise is very important. It will help you to find your Life Purpose.

◆ In your mind focus on the cell and ask what you need to know to fulfil your destiny, your Life Purpose. Ask these questions and allow the answers to flow easily to your mind.

What is that tiny cell here to do? What is it here to achieve?
What do I need to know to fulfil my path?
What is the next step I need to take on my soul journey?
What do I need to put behind me in order to move forward?

What is my special role, my part to play in the divine plan of the universe?

What is my biggest block?

How can I overcome it?

As you look at that tiny cell, the beginning of you, know that within that cell is the potential to be great, to be happy and successful, to love and be loved, to be healthy and strong and to make the world a better place. It is all there within that one tiny cell. Each and every day you make choices; those choices shape who you have become today.

....

Coincidences and Cosmic Energy

As you find you connect with the universe, the Cosmic Energy, answers will come easily to you. There is also a little gift; coincidences are the universe's way of telling us we are on the right track. We are in the flow, we are connected to Cosmic Energy.

I believe there are coincidences around us all the time to guide us. But when someone is not connected to the universal energy, and following their Life Purpose, they don't see these synchronicities or signs. You could almost trip over these signs but then complain you don't get enough spiritual guidance.

I once went to see a kinesiologist who used muscle testing to discover I needed sulphur. When she told me this, my jaw dropped – I had just come back from a road trip across Louisiana, America. After several days on the road we had suddenly come to a halt on a dusty road in the middle of nowhere with traffic backing up for miles. Eventually a ranger came up to us and said, 'Hey folks, you can either get off at the next town, travel down back roads, or sit here for two days. We have a serious chemical spill.'

It was dusk and not knowing the area or any other routes, we decided to take the next turnoff for the nearest town and find a motel for the night. The town we arrived in was called Sulphur, named because the soil there is rich in sulphur. We had nearly missed staying there, because when we asked someone on the street if there was a motel, she turned her back and ignored us. We promptly left town and headed for the next one – but got lost and ended up right back in Sulphur, which actually turned out to be a delightful little place.

Looking back I can see the universe was giving me a message – it had drawn me to the place that was rich in the very mineral I needed to dramatically improve my health. So when my kinesiologist, Isabelle, told me sulphur was what I needed, a light went on and I said, 'Ah, so that is why we kept ending up there.'

Once you acknowledge and listen to coincidences and their messages you will find them happening more frequently. It's like having the universe tap you on the shoulder when it wants to alert you to something. It's the universe's way of letting you know you are on the right track.

How does this link in with your Life Purpose? When you are lost, coincidences, universal clues, or synchronicity as some people prefer to call them, will nudge you back to your soul purpose, your Life Path. The key to coincidences is to notice when they are around – it shows you are in the flow and that the universe has an important message for you.

Notice when they are absent – maybe you are not on track.

Universal Clues

There are universal clues that tell us when we are on the right path and fulfilling our Life Purpose. It is the strangest yet simplest phenomena.

Let me give you an example. You have just come across a leaflet informing you of a workshop. Now if this workshop is relevant to your growth, one of two things (sometimes even both) will happen. You may either keep finding pennies or white feathers. It never fails to amaze me how many pennies I find when I am looking at a new project that is right for me.

The penny and feather syndrome happens all over the world in the relevant currencies, and if you learn to recognise this symbol you are well on the way to finding life easier. If it happens to you please pick the coin up – you must let the universe know you accept this gift. Remember that old saying, 'See a penny, pick it up and all the day you'll have good luck.' Well, it's true!

Look Out for the Signs

◆ At times of great stress, signs are everywhere. The universe watches over us and gives us all the tools we need to progress through adversity.

◆ In times of trauma take note of the people who are sent to you. Often it is someone who has had the very same problem except they are further down the road and can reassure you they have now got their life back – better than before.

◆ We may come across books, TV programmes or hear radio shows by 'accident'.

The universe is also marvellous at sending us someone, such as a new partner, to help us move on. I have never met anyone yet who, given time, isn't glad they had walked away from a dead relationship into a new one.

However, sometimes during difficult times you will make up with your spouse and go on to have a new awareness of how important the relationship is to you. Everyone agrees that difficult times teach them a valuable lesson – or have made them take action and pushed them in the right direction. Sometimes, it's hard to see the silver lining, but with time and reflection it will appear to you.

There's a litmus test I do with my clients. Once they have overcome their crisis I ask them, 'Would you have searched so hard or taken action if this crisis had never happened?' They always say, 'No.'

I then ask, 'How much have you learnt?' The answer again is usually along the lines of, 'masses' or 'loads'.

Next I enquire, 'How do you now feel?' And the response is, 'Oh, I'm a different person.'

It's the difficult times in our lives that show us how connected we are to the universal force. At such times, if we stay in flow and don't get dragged down by the situation we resolve our problems quickly and almost seem to be rewarded.

This next case study illustrates the subtlety of the universe and how messages, universal clues, can nudge you back in the right direction of your Life Purpose.

Case Study

One client, an architect called Joanne, was bullied at work by her boss. No matter what she did, it was never good enough.

She says, 'The boss used to shout at me in the open-plan office. She used to call me at home – one night at 11pm – to discuss work ideas and if I was off sick she would ring me up to five times a day with questions about office issues. My workload was considerably greater than my colleagues' and I was given no thanks for working late to complete it.

'However, my work was often praised by the MD, I met tight deadlines and I was known to be efficient and organised. However, because of my immediate boss slowly but surely the sparkle I had for my chosen profession began to disappear. I dreaded going into work and I felt physically sick walking into the office building.

'Then something funny happened. I heard from a colleague that the company was looking for a handful of voluntary redundancies. I really wanted to go for it and go freelance but I was scared. On the train on the way home that night I was thinking about it and noticed that a newspaper was open and there was a big headline, "How to be your own boss". Minutes later I was still asking myself, "Do I have what it takes to be self-employed?" Then I asked the universe, "If I am supposed to leave my work, please give me a sign." Within five seconds the train whizzed passed a yard full of signs, stop signs, road signs, warning triangles, you name it – there were dozens of them propped up in the yard. I took that as a sign to go for it!

'Within days I began to see the redundancy as my get-out-of-jail card, and it couldn't have come at a better time. There was no way that I was going to ignore this open door from the universe, this nudge, so I applied and I was given a great redundancy package. I believe this was the universe's way of giving me a helping hand and a great cushion while I set myself up freelance.

'I'm now very happy and earn triple my previous salary – and just when I needed it the universe provided me with a new direction, and a clear universal clue. I work on social housing, rather than big corporate contracts, and I feel that I am really putting something back in to local communities. I love my job and I feel like I'm following my Life Path by creating healthy and beautiful environments for people to live in.'

While your situation may not be as extreme as Joanne's, there are many ways that life can throw you off balance. When this happens you won't feel happy and it will have the knock-on effect of draining your energy so you won't be able to focus and achieve your Life Purpose. By identifying your Life-purpose ratio you will be able to see the areas in which you need to put in some more time, thought and/or action.

What is Your Life-purpose Ratio?

Find out just how balanced you are right now. Write down next to each area of your life the ratio of how fulfilled you feel (using 1 to 100, 100 being fulfilled). Do it quickly without thinking, as this way you will be connecting to your higher self, a part of the Cosmic Energy, and you will gain more accurate answers.

Love:

Work:

Finances:

Health:

Fun:

Friendships:

Peace of mind:

Contribution to society:

Life Purpose:

There are no right and wrong ratios. The aim of this exercise is to help you look at areas of your life and to see where you need to regain some balance, or more input – especially in the area of Life Purpose. Do you feel like you are doing what you were born to do? Answer this question honestly.

Now, you know which areas you need to focus on. Life is about trying to create harmony, balance, the yin, the yang. As well as fulfilling your potential, your role, this is another life task we all struggle with – the pursuit of inner balance. If you feel lost about how you can create balance in your life you could try meditating and taking a journey into 'you' (see also my introduction to meditation in Chapter 2, page 30).

You don't think you need to meditate? I truly believe that unless you are 100 per cent happy with your lot in life – that unless all areas such as love, work, health, finances, purpose are all 100 per cent positive – then you need to meditate. Have you ever met 'spiritual' people who tell you they have learnt it all, done it all and now have the movie rights? I like to ask the question, 'How do you know if you have learnt it all?' The answer is this – if you are still here, you still have stuff to learn.

If you have watched some old martial arts movies there is

often a scene where the master gets the novice to cut grass or paint a fence as a form of meditation. Usually the novice gets angry after a while and wonders what he or she can possibly learn from this task. The master knows that these mundane acts such as painting or walking allow our vibration to calm down, get rid of the debris and connect us to our inner selves.

One way you can meditate and connect to Cosmic Energy – and get rid of the debris in your mind – is through a walking meditation that I call 'the Journey to Self'. You can do this in the park, walking on the beach or walking round your local reservoir. Sylvia is disabled but still does the Journey to Self. She sits at home and imagines she is walking down a leafy lane. She allows her mind to flow and often can smell the flowers and feel a breeze as the answers come to her.

Many people find it difficult to meditate. They get distracted and annoyed with their lack of concentration. But by taking a strolling meditation you will eliminate many of the problems associated with meditation in the usual sense.

The Journey to Self – A Walking Meditation

1. Decide where you can walk between ten and thirty minutes a day. Find somewhere that is right for you.

2. Decide on your walking place and allow your mind to flow for the first few minutes. You may find yourself thinking about what you need to do, things you have forgotten to do, maybe a letter you should have posted. Tell yourself that for a short while you will put all this aside, but will come back to it and deal with it all in a while.

3. Keep walking and allow your arms to swing by your side at the same pace as your steps. Now allow your breathing to also match the pace. Concentrate on breathing in and out to the rhythm of your steps and arm swings.

   Walking creates a flow and as you flow you will find the vibration that allows your inner self to activate and connect with what is best for you.

   The flow created by gently strolling is similar to the flow of a river, and as the river flows the debris falls to the bottom allowing the surface of the water to become clear, and so the same will happen with your thoughts.

4. As you walk, focus on what you need to know. It can be a specific question such as:

   ◆ Am I working in the right place?

   ◆ Or it can be more abstract, such as 'Is there anything I am meant to be doing with my life?'

   ◆ Is there anything important for me to know?

   There is not a right or wrong way to do this meditation. The questions don't have to be terribly worthy, if there is something you need to know then just ask it.

5. As you stroll notice what thoughts, feelings and impressions flow to you. Do not censor them or feel they are wrong. Do not judge; let the thoughts flow.

6. Focus on your breathing, which connects the outer world to the inner you. It will bring your day-to-day world to the deeper part of you.

You may find yourself suddenly thinking about things that have happened in your childhood or distant past. This may be a message that your dilemma now has its roots in the past. If so, imagine leaving the past situation by the wayside as you carry on strolling and know that you have moved beyond it.

There's a saying, 'Take time to stop and smell the flowers on the way' and this Journey to Self can help you do this, taking time out for you and connecting you with Cosmic Energy.

People often tell me they do not have time for this exercise. I ask them how long they spend each day watching television, texting, sending jokes over the internet or looking at unimportant websites. They always look slightly embarrassed. Anyone can find ten minutes a day to stroll and think.

Top Tips For Getting the Most Out of Your Journey to Self

◆ Do not try too hard – simply focus on what you need to know then allow your mind to flow.

◆ If you get distracted or if your mind wanders, simply say the word 'back' then bring your mind back to the subject.

◆ Do not worry if nothing much happens at first – often the information is being processed. Then the answer will come when you least expect it.

◆ Be patient. You may get an answer in minutes, but it can take days, months or even years. The answer will come when it comes.

◆ Do not judge your answer – allow it to flow.

◆ Do not try to answer every question in the world. Just focus on one important question.

Buddha Bar

Buddha was working behind a bar when a man walked in and asked him for a bottle of beer. He handed Buddha a large note and waited for Buddha to hand him back some money, but he didn't. Eventually the man said to Buddha, 'Hey, buddy, where is my change?' and Buddha replied, 'My friend, don't you know that all change is within?'

The Bigger Picture

While you are walking the Journey to Self, you may ask yourself the question, 'Why am I here?' or 'What is life all about?' By asking these questions you will discover your Life Purpose. I believe our existence here on earth is like an apprenticeship – each day you learn and the quicker you learn, the easier life becomes.

We all lead fragile lives, just like spring blossom – a blast of wind in the shape of an unexpected problem or trauma can scatter the petals and leave the tree bare. Even when life is pretty good, you can spend your time worrying (even if the worries are just at the back of your mind).

At times it is difficult to believe the universe has our best interests at heart. We've all had bleak episodes when nothing goes right and a big black cloud seems to hover above us. We feel as if we are aimlessly wandering through life without purpose, but then we search for answers, which are hopefully not too far away.

Tough times occur when we stray from our Life Purpose and only by feeling down do we search for the answers that bring us back onto the right path. Maybe, also, there is a lesson you need to learn? You are free to go on searching until you find a new way, a new Life Path. You can find this Life Path through quiet contemplation and by listening to what's inside your heart.

Now we have established how to find your Life Path we can look at connecting on a wider scale, to the universe, the world and to our fellow human beings.

CHAPTER 7
Inner Self

Most people tend to see themselves as lone entities, separate from others and separate from the universe, a view of the self fed by the ego. Yet once we begin to realise that we are part of everything, and everyone, life becomes easier. In this chapter I'm going to help you to break free of your ego and connect to your inner self, the inner part of you that is linked to the Cosmic Energy all around us. When you are connected, you can link in and blend with the natural flow. You can become part of everything, and when you do, the ego vanishes and you gain strength. This is because once you know that you are part of something whole and great, you realise your own power.

This chapter will focus on how you can:

1. Connect with the universe

2. Connect with other people

Connect with the Universe

As we already talked about in Chapter 2, ancient peoples were connected to the universe. They listened to omens and dreams and followed their instincts. They were connected to each other, to their tribe – and had to be, otherwise they wouldn't have survived. Then as society 'progressed', the connections between us and the Cosmic Energy around us were lost. Now, little by little, people are beginning to realise that the things they desire separate them from others, from the earth, from the universe and from themselves. This desire comes from the ego.

What is Ego?

The ego is the 'I', the voice in your head that talks about its desires and fears. In psychoanalysis it is referred to as the 'conscious mind' that meditates on your surroundings and gives a constant commentary on what the 'I' thinks. Think about it: when you walk into a party, you have a voice in your head that passes comment on what is happening. The voice, the ego, may say something like, 'Everyone is looking at me', or when you are out shopping you may think, 'I want that pair of shoes.' Whatever the message relating to your desires and fears, this is your ego talking. The ego worries what others think. It worries that you are not good enough or that you will fail. It chatters endlessly about what it wants, where it wants to be, and it is never satisfied.

The ego leads to negative ways of attempting to raise your energy with alcohol, tobacco, drugs, shopping and overeating.

The ego creates negative behaviour to bolster it into feeling better than those around you. It likes to score points off others, it tries to prove itself by saying, 'Look at me, I am clever, popular, nicer, kinder . . .'

The ego gains a temporary boost by buying things. It tells the world, 'I must be someone because look at my car, jewellery, sofa, house.' It constantly demands attention. It gains attention by being too nice or even aggressive. It boasts, it's defensive and it's fragile. One little criticism can send the ego into a downward emotional spiral.

By realising that you are connected to everything and every-body you can begin to lead your life in the right way – move away from your ego and connect with your Inner Self, and fulfil your Life Purpose. You will not need others to validate you.

As we have seen, if you become more aware of your Cosmic Energy you will begin to realise that the energy and thoughts you send out will come back to you more powerfully, which is why if someone treats you badly you shrug because you know that it's simply a reflection of how they see themselves and their world. In fact, one of the most useful ways to connect with the world is to learn to shrug. Most things that annoy people deserve just a shrug. When you learn not to buy into the everyday dramas and worries of those around you, you come out of the ego and connect with your universal self, the Cosmic Energy that is within all of us.

When I teach my clients about the ego in workshops, I tell them this story. I first heard the tale in Calcutta, told to me by Vikram, one of my first mentors. Only in recent times have I realised just how important its message was.

Vikram's Story

One day a carpet seller was travelling from town to town trying to sell his wares. On the back of his donkey were the finest silk carpets, but try as hard as he might he could not sell a single rug. He despaired as his money ran out, and his thoughts turned to his family awaiting his return with the big bag of golden coins he had promised them.

As night drew near, he fell asleep at the foot of a mountain. In his dreams a voice told him that the mountain had a message for him and that he needed to ask what that message was, because it would help him.

The carpet seller awoke at dawn and looked around him. He looked at the mountain and making sure there was no one about he said softly, 'What is the message you have for me?' He waited but no reply came. He repeated his question a little louder: 'What is the message you have for me?' Again, no reply came.

Feeling foolish, the carpet seller sat down but in his desperation he decided to ask one more time. This time he stood up straight, faced the mountain and shouted, 'What is the message you have for me?' Immediately his words echoed back at him: 'What is the message you have for me?' He stood flummoxed – now the mountain was asking him the same question.

He tried again, this time bellowing his question, and again the question came bellowing back. The carpet seller grew angry and shouted, 'Why do you mock me?'. The echo retorted, 'Why do you mock me?' Furious, he yelled, 'You are foolish!' The echo came back: 'You are foolish!'

The carpet seller went on his way. Upset and angry, he came upon a tiny tea house and spent the last of his money on tea and a piece of bread. He looked around the tea house and noticed how it was warm and richly furnished. The carpet seller wondered how a simple tea seller could live so well, so he asked him how he could live so richly. He found himself telling the tea seller about the mountain and how it had mocked him.

The tea seller told him, 'I too came upon a mountain and it gave me a very special message, which is why I live so well today.'

The carpet seller was curious and asked him what the message was. The tea seller told him, 'All mountains carry a special message. The mountain is simply showing you how everything you do and say is echoed back to you. Your lack of success has simply been a reflection of the things you have said and done regarding yourself and others.'

The carpet seller sat and thought and realised that he often wished people ill luck and thought everyone was a fool. The carpet seller reached the next town with a smile on his face, imagining the people there to be warm and happy souls who would love a beautiful carpet in their homes.

He returned home with a bag of gold, having sold all his carpets. But he had also learnt the most important lesson of his life from a very special message from a mountain.

The Power of the Breath, the Life Force

As a psychic, I am blessed with the gift of being able to see people's energy fields. I can see the colours and shapes coming off their body, which are fascinating to observe. I often sit outside coffee shops and watch the world pass by. It's interesting to see just how many people show signs of stress. It looks almost like interference on a TV screen – sometimes like sparks flying off them, or as jagged flashes of energy in their auras. It's easy to see that their minds are working overtime with worry.

As I began to study people I knew, I found that some had more sparks than others. When people have more stress, there are more sparks, but every so often I see someone who, no matter what was going on in their life, seems to have fewer sparks than others. There is something calm about their energy field.

Now there is something else interesting that I observed about the people I came into contact with as clients or through everyday life. Somehow those who had virtually no sparks resolved their problems really quickly. Often these were high-powered people with companies to run or very busy lives with unexpected situations to deal with on a daily basis. Yet somehow their energy field stayed calm and problems soon evaporated.

My curiosity led me to ask them why they felt their lives were somehow easier or calmer. Again and again they would tell me that they never doubted that things would turn out well, no matter how bad it looked at the time. They also didn't moan or relay tales of horror to all and sundry – they just quietly dealt with the problem at hand, without overly discussing the situation except when necessary with people who would help deal with the issue. By taking this approach, they didn't create more drama and therefore didn't feed the problem with more energy.

I began to probe more deeply and found that in every case, bar one, these high-powered calm people all did something that balanced their energy, such as meditation (especially transcendental meditation), yoga or tai chi. Somehow these disciplines connect us to the universal frequency, to Cosmic Energy, and people who practice such disciplines have a still inner self. They can centre themselves and go within when things get tough; and this reflects on how they interact with their world, in turn creating a calmer energy around them.

Jack, a company manager, demonstrated this perfectly. Here is his story.

Case Study

Jack was always frantic about something. Most days he was on the telephone to complaints departments and call centres. He always seemed to have something to complain about, his car breaking down, machinery malfunctioning at his factory and staff problems.

Jack told me, 'I would probably have continued forever like that if it wasn't for a check-up.' Jack's company decided to introduce health insurance and the terms were that the staff had to have a health check-up. Jack had always been very healthy and was pretty shocked when the doctor told him he was close to a heart attack unless he lost weight and brought his blood pressure down.

His wife took control of the situation and made him walk daily. She oversaw what he ate and drank and dragged him with her to yoga. Jack was mortified at first but soon had to admit, 'I had the best night's sleep ever after the first class.'

When there was an upheaval at work a few weeks later, instead of going off the deep end ranting and raving Jack relaxed and handled the situation. The upheaval was a recurring problem, but after his calm approach it never happened again. Jack is convinced that doing yoga changed his energy. The old Jack attracted problems, but the new Jack has a serene, problem-free vibration. During times of trouble he can go within and draw on his inner self's strength, the life force within, and his inner calm.

Yoga, tai chi and meditation allow your frequency to settle into a softer but somehow stronger vibration. They also help you to align and connect with universal energy, enabling you to find the right solutions quickly. So instead of frantically running around in circles, you remain calm and connected, and deal swiftly with the situation.

Jack told me, 'Now instead of exploding with anger I find myself thinking, "Right, how can I resolve this problem?" My workers can hardly believe the change in me. My wife is also delighted because I'm now a lot calmer at home too.'

Jack's story highlights how what we give out comes back. I also want to emphasise that every moment of every day you are surrounded by energy of all kinds, from people, objects, places, emotions. Everything that happens leaves an energy imprint. By raising your vibration and connecting with Cosmic Energy most vibrations will pass you by, especially those that cause problems or make you feel unsettled.

In the following pages are the main things I have found to enhance and settle personal vibrations and create a calmer you. There are many forms of chi jung martial arts and various methods of breathing that will connect you with the universe, the life force, so do experiment and find the one which resonates with you.

Once you start to practise regularly you will clear any chaotic energy you have as residue from past problems. You will align your mind and body with the universal force and create a peaceful inner self – so the voice in your head that normally chatters about what it desires and feels will be quieter and talk less frequently. Most everyday problems and difficulties will flow straight past you, but any issues that come your way can be easily resolved. One of my clients even found she got fewer parking tickets. She told me, 'I drive all over London and at times have to park on double yellow lines. I used to average a parking ticket a fortnight, but now I doubt I get one every two months. I even saw one traffic warden check every car along the road except for mine.'

The Best Ways to Connect With the Universe

All of these practices promote a sense of calm, which you will find when the chattering stops. This helps you access your inner peace and space – a direct link to the universe.

Yoga

Yoga goes back thousands of years and is basically a series of body postures, breathing exercises and concentration techniques that align your mind, body and spirit. Most people spend their lives in either their minds or their bodies, or way up in their heads in their spiritual selves. How often do you connect to all three? You may focus too much in your body and work too hard, or think too much and live in your head. And we have all met spiritual people who seem to live with their head in the clouds! Yoga aligns all three (mind, body and spirit) so chi flows freely. When this happens you slow down your thinking and allow the universal messages to flow to you.

Yoga makes your body stronger and more flexible.
It calms your mind and lifts your spirits bringing clarity.
It connects your earthly self with your spiritual self.

Tai Chi

Tai chi and qigong (a form of tai chi) have a similar effect to yoga. You may have seen Chinese people in parks practising tai chi and have noted the graceful moves and peaceful looks on their faces.

I practise qigong under the watchful eyes of John Solagbade, a true master. I met John when he came to see me for a reading and as soon we shook hands I thought, 'I must train with this man.' I later went along to John Solagbade's monthly class. As I watched him performing the slow moves, he had an air of serenity and poise. I asked him how anyone could defend themselves with such graceful movements. Without a word, and in what seemed like less than a second, he did the moves he had been teaching us with such speed and sharpness there was a swishing noise in the air – the power was colossal. He then continued with his gentle movements.

John says, 'Qigong, literally translated is "energy (qi) skill (gong)" or "the art of cultivating the qi", works by gently synchronising one's conscious intent, breathing and precise movements of the body. There are many forms of qigong; tai chi is one such form.'

I asked him how it could affect the body. He told me, 'It centres the qi in the lower abdominal, which is the body's intrinsic reservoir of universal energy, and promotes its free and harmonious circulation throughout the body.'

John trained under Grandmaster Chen Xiao Wang, who always emphasised the importance of correct posture because this allows qi to circulate freely. Blocked qi produces disharmony and negative emotional states such as anger, while flowing qi brings us back to our natural state of harmony, contentment and joy. The motto on his logo is 'HEART OF JOY'.

I asked John how such a gentle exercise could be so powerful. He answered that the meditative aspects allow you to remain calm and clear in the heat of threat, actual or perceived.

When I first started training in qigong I wanted to know if it could connect a person to the universal energy. John told me, 'Yes, qi is universal energy. By improving its flow through the body, heart-mind and consciousness, one becomes increasingly able to perceive the ever-present connection with universal energy; which is what we are! Qi is the equivalent of 'the Force' in the Star Wars saga, and, it requires conscious cultivation.'

Case Study

Horst Rainer Worz, sixty, suffered two back seizures each year for ten years. Each time he was bedridden and in excruciating pain for up to two weeks. One day eighteen years ago Catharine, his physiotherapist, suggested he tried qigong. Providence was smiling on him because that week there had been an article on a qigong class in a local magazine – so he signed up.

For the last twelve years Horst has worked six days a week doing 'man and van' deliveries, which involve lots of heavy lifting. He says, 'I am happy and vigorous and think nothing of the weekly five-hour round trip for a four-hour class of qigong. It has such a positive impact on my health and keeps the back seizures at bay, so it really is worth the long drive.'

Since then, thanks to his regular practice, Horst has only had two seizures in the last eighteen years, both of which where of short duration and low intensity. Horst recalls, 'The first seizure happened because I laid a foundation of huge concrete paving slabs and built my garden shed all in one day, and the second I was involved in lots of heavy lifting and didn't take a break! I was foolish, I pushed my body too hard.'

Tens of millions of people in China practise tai chi. In separate experiments conducted in Australia and Taiwan, diabetes patients who performed tai chi for a few hours per week over a three-month period showed significant health improvement. Given my own first-hand experiences of the benefits of qigong, I'm not surprised that clinical trials are showing what practitioners have known for thousands of years: tai chi is good for you – as is breathing properly.

Breathing in Cosmic Energy

You take your first breath as you enter your life and your last as you leave. Breathing is your connection from your universal self to your earthly self. Many people often forget this and, instead of valuing their breathing, they shallow-breathe, taking in a small amount of the universal energy that keeps them connected and alive.

By learning to breathe in Cosmic Energy you can quickly go into an altered state, calm down and connect your mind and body to the universal force. Each breath you take is like charging a battery, but good breathing charges the battery deeper and for longer. The better you breathe the more cells you energise, and the better the connection to the universal force. It's like having good reception on your mobile phone. When the connection is weak you cut out and cannot connect properly. By consciously breathing, you are consciously bringing chi into your body.

I am now going to teach you how to use breathing to bring Cosmic Energy into your body, which will also help clear your mind and help you cope with stress.

The Cosmic Breath Technique

◆ Simply lie quietly and focus on your breathing. The quieter your environment, the better. As you breathe in be aware of the universal breath flowing into you, energising every cell of your body. As you breathe out, feel any old stale energy flow away.

◆ Now breathe in through your nose and out through your mouth, breathing from your abdomen – actually feel your tummy rise and fall. Put one hand on your abdomen and feel this movement, breathing in then breathing out. Know as you do this you are connecting to the universal force.

◆ Feel the breath energise your body and calm your mind. Feel your mind becoming clearer and calmer. Feel the Cosmic Energy flowing through your body.

Here are other ways you can use your breath, such as giving yourself a burst of energy or creating a sense of calm to help with stressful situations.

◆ **Breath balancer**
At odd moments during the day, stop and fill your lungs with air, hold for a few seconds then slowly release. This will align your mind, body and spirit, when your thoughts are running away with you, for example.

◆ **Stress buster**
If you are feeling stressed or worried or have tension in your body, stop and focus on your breathing. Breathe in through

your nose and out through your mouth and as you do so, hum. Make this a definite and strong hum that vibrates – this will give you an immediate feeling of calm as it releases any tension.

♦ **Wakey wakey**

To stimulate your mind and body or if you are simply feeling tired or run down, this exercise will perk you up. Take very quick, short breaths in and out, almost like panting. Aim for two breathes in and out per second. This acts like bellows on a fire, rapidly bringing vibrancy to your body and mind. Do this for no more than ten seconds.

♦ **Body balancer**

Use the walking meditation, as described in the previous chapter (see page 199). As you walk, match your breathing to your walking pace, maybe two or three breaths per step, or whatever you find comfortable. This balances out your entire body and can particularly help you to feel more grounded, especially if your life has been out of balance.

Meditation

Like yoga and tai chi, meditation is another excellent way to connect with Cosmic Energy (see also the meditation section in Chapter 2, page 30).

The Power of Thought

In 1972, twenty-four cities in the United States with populations over ten thousand took part in a study that aimed to use meditation to create inner peace and reduce violence in society. As few as one per cent of the population took part in the study, which saw participants meditating on specific days of each month and at specific times.

On the days when participants meditated, the crime rate in those cities was 16 per cent lower than normal. This effect became known as the 'Maharishi Effect' after the Maharishi Mahesh yogi who said that when one per cent of the population practised the meditation he taught, there would be a reduction in violence and crime in that area.

Dr David Edwards, professor of Government, University of Texas at Austin, commented, 'I think the claim can be plausibly made that the potential impact of this research exceeds that of any other ongoing social or psychological research programme. It has survived a broader array of statistical tests than most research in the field of conflict resolution. This work and the theory that informs it deserve the most serious consideration by academics and policy makers alike.'

Another experiment, the 'International Peace Project in the Middle East' was published in the *Journal of Conflict Resolution* in 1988. The experiment took place during the Israeli-Lebanese war in the early 1980s. Those taking part used meditation to create peace in their bodies rather than simply thinking about it or asking for it to occur.

On specific days at specific times, participants were positioned within the war-torn areas of the Middle East. During these times

crime, car accidents, emergency hospital visits, and terrorist inci-
dents all declined. When they stopped the experiment, the
figures reversed to the normal higher rates.

The benefits of meditation make a very long list, from lower
stress and blood pressure levels to less depression and better
decision-making. But to also know that meditation affects the
world around us makes me think that the next time any of us
says we are too busy to meditate, we need to ask ourselves this:
what else is so important that we cannot manage ten minutes a
day to change the world?

Martial Arts

Many of the martial arts also align the mind, body and spirit.
You will know when you have found your teacher; they will
have something about them that draws you to them.

A few years ago I had neighbours who described themselves
as 'martial arts teachers'. They slumped in and out of the
building. They were rude, sullen and had terrible postures. A
true master has a gentle but perfect poise, an air of happiness
and calm, perfect manners and control. Look out for these
qualities when choosing your sensei (martial arts teacher).

As you practise any of the disciplines such as yoga, qigong and
martial arts you will become aware of sensations in your mind
and body. It may be a tingle or warmth; it may be a focus on a
certain area. You may be aware of a lightness or heaviness on your
body, or a sensation moving from one area to another, or
spreading outwards. These are all signs that you are energising
your chi and, over time, you will be able to move and control it.

You will also find that while you are breathing, meditating or performing yoga or tai chi, you suddenly have a flash of inspiration or clarity. Or you may suddenly let go of something that was previously bothering you. These are all signs that you are aligning your own energy with that of the universe, the Cosmic Energy. You are connecting to your true essence, your inner self, and the calmness within all of us.

Connect with Other People

If I needed to get a mass of people all aligned and working together, or groups of people to come together instead of pulling apart or even fighting, I would use sound and music. Watch footage of huge concerts, and you see tens of thousands of people all moving in synchronicity to the sound of their idol, unified in moving to the same sound, the same beat connecting them. Just one person can create something that will influence hundreds of thousands of people; words float into our brains from songs and stay there indefinitely.

How often have you heard a song on the radio that you have not heard in many years, yet immediately begin to sing along to it? You know the words – they have been stored in your brain all that time.

Our ancient selves also knew about the powerful force of sound, which is why they used sacred sound – mantras – and had great acoustics in temples and churches. Music is regaining some of its ancient power. One kind of dance music is known as trance because it takes the dancers into an altered state – it vibrates on the base and heart chakra, creating a feeling of primal love and connection. It gives the feeling of tribal music.

I asked London DJ Ben Harrington why music had such a powerful and profound effect on people. I will let him answer:

'Music is the expression of someone's creative thoughts and that's why good musicians/singers/DJs/artists/bands are so well received. We're creating magic! I've seen rooms, venues, and fields of people moving in unity to loud, thumping hypnotising beats – and it's awesome, especially from the view of the DJ booth. I have to vibe off the audience; feel their presence through observing behaviours and reactions. How are they feeling? What do they want to feel? Then I select my song, my ... "tool", and push the vibe back to them: "TAKE THIS!" ... And I observe more.

'It's absolutely amazing how the "vibe" of a song can play with a crowd. One tune will have hands in the air with smiling faces everywhere, then the next will have heads down, bodies in a trance-like state.'

The next time you need to influence a group of people, use music – perhaps when you are having a few friends over for dinner, when teaching, or whenever you want to cheer someone up or calm them down. Experiment and notice how you can change the whole vibration of a room just by selecting certain genres of music. Play with ideas; notice what people start to talk about as the music changes. I often find Japanese music makes people quite sentimental, Celtic music makes people smile and become more playful. Violins seem to stir memories and pianos make people creative.

The following exercise, Earth Watch, is good for helping you connect with other people. If possible, do it outside. I have done this in my garden, in a group on a large lawn and on a rooftop. I have also practised this in my office and bedroom. All the venues work very well, but there is something about being outside and/or doing this in a group that makes it particularly exhilarating.

Earth Watch

◆ Stand straight with your feet firmly on the ground, shoulders broad and open, and legs shoulder width apart. Breathe comfortably and evenly and feel any stress flow from you, down and out through the soles of your feet. Spend a few moments connecting with your breathing, clearing your mind and releasing stress into the ground beneath you.

◆ Take a deep breath and imagine yourself floating up into the air, higher and higher into the sky. Look down at the houses, stream and roads as you float higher and higher into the sky then out of the earth's atmosphere ... higher and higher, further and further you go out into the universe. As you float out feel yourself connected and strong in the universe.

◆ Now feel the universe becoming smaller and smaller. As the universe becomes smaller you feel bigger and stronger and more powerful. You are standing tall in the universe and it shrinks around you. You look around and everything is so much closer and clearer.

◆ You are standing tall in the universe, so tall that the planets are spinning past you. Watch in wonderment as the planets float by in all their breathtaking beauty – the redness of Mars, the prettiness of Venus. And in front of you, the size of a tennis ball, is a beautiful little ball. Your home, the planet earth. So lush, so deep, so special.

This planet is the home to so many people, people you love and know and those you will never meet. It's home to so many animals, insects, birds, plants, trees and fish. There is so much of everything on that little planet. So small against the rest of the universe.

◆ As it floats past you, reach out and pick up the beautiful planet earth in the palm of your hand. You look down on the oceans, mountains, rain forests and cities. You watch little clouds floating above its surface.

Look down on planet earth and know just how very special this little planet is and how much you love it.

◆ Feel your Etheric Energy build up in your hands just as you learnt to do earlier (see the Etheric Energy Technique, Chapter 2, page 34). And as you hold planet earth, send a blast of pure energy to its centre. Know that the earth is soaking up the energy and gratefully receives it. Feel yourself giving back energy to the earth that has sustained you, kept you strong, given air to breathe, water to drink and food to eat. The earth that has given you so much.

◆ Continue sending planet earth pure energy, and now send pure unconditional love to the planet earth, your home. Feel the love and Etheric Energy reach right down to its very core and feel the earth becoming stronger, healthier, cleaner and happier and more powerful.

◆ The earth has now absorbed all the energy you have sent. When you are ready, give planet earth a little push with your hands to send it back into orbit.

◆ Feel the universe growing back to its usual size and now float back down to planet earth. Feel your feet firmly back on the ground. Feel the connection with your planet and feel the love between the earth and you. Now you are the earth, and the earth is you. You are one. You will always know this, and this knowledge will keep your energy strong, powerful and safe for all time.

....

I did this exercise with a large group in London in a secluded park. At the time I wasn't sure how the participants had got on with it as they all seemed quite subdued afterwards. About one week later, however, I began to get emails from them telling me how they had felt.

One particular participant stood out. This email came from Timothy, a painfully shy man who always seemed so lost and struggling with life. He wrote, 'Anne, I just wanted to thank you so much for the earth energy exercise we did last Saturday. Somehow I used to feel as if I didn't belong in this world, I always felt so out of place. Now, something in me has changed, I have made friends, chatted to people at work (I never do normally). I even popped into a pub and had a pint and talked to strangers who were friendly to me. I don't know why it has changed me so much, all I can think is that it has somehow made me feel that I am part of everything that is here and that I deserve my place. I am meant to be here. A chap at work even asked me what I had done. I asked him what he meant and he said, "Well, you look quite pleased with yourself, just different somehow." He is right – I am different. I feel happy and connected to myself and those around me.'

The more we connect to each other and with Cosmic Energy the better life becomes for us, and as an added bonus we help make the world a better place. When we connect with others we begin to notice our similarities instead of our differences. We gain empathy for each other and support each other.

By spending a few minutes a day practising the exercises in this book you will not only notice a difference in your own life, but will also make a difference to the lives of others and to the world.

EPILOGUE

Your Journey of Happiness Starts Now

In this busy world, it's easy to lose track of what is important, to lose your connection with Cosmic Energy and get waylaid by gadgets and toys, finding magic in remote controls and jet engines. Yet the real magic is all around you, every moment of every day. And this energy, this chi, is just waiting for you to tap into it and work with it.

Luckily, people now are reawakening to this knowledge and by using the tools and exercises in this book, you too can begin to find out just how wonderful Cosmic Energy is and how you can harness it to manifest the life you deserve, to manifest your happiness.

In Chapter 2 you discovered the tools of Cosmic Energy. Many of these came from our ancient selves and have been used for hundreds, if not thousands, of years. You learnt how to use these tools and understand their specific benefits, and also how to combine various tools for a powerful synergistic effect in any area of your life.

In Chapter 3, on love and relationships, we examined how some people are unlucky in relationships yet others attract great love. I have shown you how you can use your own energy to overcome relationship problems and rekindle a flagging relationship, and even how to manifest the perfect partner. I hope you will take the techniques from this chapter and use them to transform your relationships so you can enjoy the love life you deserve.

In Chapter 4 we looked at how you can attract wealth and overcome a negative poverty consciousness, which may have been blocking your abundance. You discovered exactly how to use the power of manifestation by using your powerful energy field, and now know how to create the right opportunities to give you financial stability. I showed you how to use an abundance funnel (see page 123) – if you are self-employed, in sales, or have to drum up business in any industry, this can bring the work and sales flooding in. The Nine Keys to Wealth (see page 113) will provide you with a stable foundation to work from and give you the elusive Midas touch. Importantly, you learnt how to rewrite your financial history so you can escape your past and look forward to a future of prosperity and stability and be free of money worries.

In Chapter 5 you discovered how to find your true vocation via numerology (Find Your Life Path With Numerology, page 150). Be brave and think about how you can use this knowledge to take the next steps on your career path – or even use it to follow your dream career. My Etheric Energy Techniques, or EETs (page 156) will help get you noticed at an interview so you need never feel too nervous again about going for a new job or promotion. You also learnt how to use EET to tap into your boss or colleagues and even take control and direct meetings, which on a basic level means avoiding hours wasted going round in circles, and in the wider scheme of things gives you more input into what is happening in your office and company.

Other topics covered in this chapter included how to astral-travel to prospective companies and clients to discover their needs, giving you the edge over your competitors, and how to create sacred space at work. A sacred space will help you to be more creative, feel safe and protected, and allow you to tap into Cosmic Energy so you can operate at work with sincerity, strength and harmony. Whatever you feel you lack, such as confidence or organisational ability, don't fret any more – you learnt how to use the ability cloaks to give you these character-istics (see Your Wardrobe of Ability Cloaks, page 173). In a harsh office space you can also use the cloaks for protection so the bullies will leave you alone and you will no longer dread going to work. Nobody should have to face this trauma, but now you know how to be free of it and take control of your working life.

Chapter 6 looked at your Life Purpose and how everything you need to know is within you. I described why some of us are given hard times in order to learn and grow, and how your own energy has survived lifetime after lifetime. We looked at how coincidences can show us the way forward and hopefully, now, you will know how to recognise these subtle signs, which can have such a big impact on your decision-making process.

The Life-purpose Ratio (see page 197) will have given you a clear picture of where you need to redress the balance in your life. Perhaps it will tell you things that your loved ones want to, but feel afraid to? It may reveal that your work has become far too important and that you need to think about how much time you spend with your family. This chapter revealed a powerful technique for meditation called the Journey to Self (see page 199) which you can use to work through problems and to connect with the deeper eternal energy that's you. Journey to

Self can also help you find answers to some of life's big questions, such as 'Why am I here?' and 'What is life all about?' These questions have been on the lips of philosophers for centuries. Now you have your own way of finding the answers.

Finally, in Chapter 7 we looked at how to overcome the ego, which along with making us all nicer people, frees you from the constant chatter of desires and wants. You learnt how to connect with the life force with the power of breath, giving you a sense of peace and contentment. Situations that cause chaos will no longer trigger anger and anxiety – you can take a step back and breathe and know that problems will be sorted out. Your new attitude will benefit you, your colleagues and your loved ones. Imagine not bringing work problems home with you, being able to separate your work and home life so work issues no longer dominate your free time. As a result, every day will seem longer – you won't be stuck on the cycle of birth, school, work, death. It will be more like birth, school, work, play, enjoyment, relaxation, fun, realising your Life Purpose and your Soul Path, then on to a higher realm!

You now know that you are so much more than your five senses. You are a being of energy connected to all the energy in the universe. You will notice when energy is dense and heavy, making life difficult, and when it is light and flowing, when things are going well and life becomes easy. You will be aware of the energy of others and how it affects you. You will be able to make quick, and better, decisions about the people you come into contact with at work and in your personal life.

As you tap into Cosmic Energy you will become stronger and part of the universal flow. Once you are in flow what you need flows easily to you. And as our bodies flow, we become healthier and stronger. As you connect with the universe you discover your true vocation, and you will know just what to do to make work doors open for you, and as you will be in the flow, the right people will appear to help you on your quest. Life becomes an adventure rather than a nightmare.

This final exercise is a favourite of mine. I often use it to end my workshops, leaving the participants feeling wonderful. Not only do you send a healing vibration out into the world, you make that vibration big and powerful. Best of all, after it has been sent that amazing feeling comes straight back to you, giving you a fabulous wave of positive and joyous energy.

Soul Smile

◆ Find yourself back on top of the mountain (see the Mystic Mountain Visualisation, Chapter 3). Feel the cool air gently touch your face. Be aware of the silence above you, the total peace of the universe. Be aware of the ground beneath your feet connecting you to your life here on earth. Notice how time has stood still and you are at one with the earth and the sky and the universe. You are at one with everyone who has ever lived, who lives right now and who will be there in the future long after you have gone.

◆ Connect with your soul energy that is deep within you, the energy that has been you lifetime after lifetime. Feel a deep happiness stir within you as you connect with the real you – your soul energy. A happiness that comes from knowing that you can make a difference to the world. You have a wonderful vital energy flowing through you that you can send out to the world and that brings joy to everyone.

◆ Feel your soul energy within you taking the form of a beautiful smile that begins deep inside you and spreads right through your body. Feel the smile spreading happiness all the way up your legs and into your abdomen, up your arms, your torso and into your neck and head. Now focus on sending out that smile to an elderly man called Charlie, he lives alone in a little bungalow. Send him out a big smile and feel it reach him. Know that your smile has made him happier and lets him know he is cared for. Now feel his face break into a big smile as he sends the smile back to you.

◆ Now send the smile to everyone on the street where he lives. Feel the residents stop for a moment, feel the smile and give a big beaming smile back to you.

◆ Send a big smile out to the whole town and feel the smile come straight back to you, feeling the warmth wash over you. As the smile reaches you, send it to the entire county – feel your smile spread over villages, towns and fields. Feel the smile flow straight back to you.

◆ Now smile at the whole country and feel your smile flowing into hospitals and schools, to prisons and court rooms, to offices and factories. Feel your smile flow to good people, feel your smile flow to grumpy people, selfish people. Feel your smile flow along rivers and roads, feel your smile reach every part of the country and feel people stopping and smiling and receiving the happiness you are sending them from the depths of your soul.

◆ Feel everyone in the land send a big smile back to you; feel the smile getting bigger and bigger and it joins with other smiles. Feel all the smiles join together into one huge smile and feel it flow right through you – a huge loving, beaming smile.

◆ Take that huge smile and send it out to the entire world. Feel it flow over mountains and rivers, across oceans and seas, to the ends of the earth and across the equator. Feel it reach rich people, poor people, people who live in apartments, houses, villas, mansions or mud huts. Feel it reach people in igloos, caravans and shacks. Feel it reach people who have nowhere to live.

Feel the smile circle the earth, spreading joy in its wake, drawing together all the souls on earth.

◆ Now pause and hear a rumble: know that right now all the souls on earth are uniting, rumbling towards you as they join together in one huge wave. Feel a smiling wave flow right over you, bringing you an exhilarating and joyful energy that flows right over you, sending you love and happiness from every single soul on earth. As the soul smile flows through you, feel it flow out through the soles of your feet and into the earth, all the way down to its very core, sending a wave of beautiful love and smiles from the people who live upon her.

Know that you can make a difference and that each time you connect with your soul energy you will send out a smile that will spread far and wide, making the world you live in a far better place.

As I found connection on top of a mountain, so you will find a sacred place that will connect you – it may be your local park, your back garden or simply somewhere in your home.

The earth is working with you. You will be attracted to the energy of your own special place, where you will find the silence that heightens your senses. You will not need to look for it. You will find yourself naturally guided to people, places and anything that helps you to connect to the universal energy.

As you feel and sense energy you will feel more alive, because energy is alive. At first the energy will be subtle, but soon it will be amplified so that you will know in an instant whether something is right for you or not.

As you become more aware you will be able to control energy and to send your own Etheric Energy out to people, places and into the universe. You will use it to get attention and to create certain moods and vibrations.

As you connect with the universal force, problems and issues that normally drag you down will no longer bother you. You will have more important things to deal with. You will rise above petty day-to-day issues, and each time you do your energy will rise even higher. You will not be at the mercy of difficult people – you will be in control of your energy and what happens in your life.

You will become aware that you are a wonderful, magnificent, powerful and wise being who has the capacity to change the world, to make a difference. You have a powerful energy running through you that has not been utilised to its full potential.

Every time you create positive energy you affect others, who in turn will affect others. One small gesture can make huge changes. Try it – stop and give a kind word to someone you do not normally speak to, the chap selling the *Big Issue*, the lady in the newsagents, the elderly person you walk past each day. Notice how they light up and in turn will be more inclined to speak to others. Try it especially with someone who is usually grumpy or difficult; find something nice to say to them.

At times your gesture may be rebuffed, but know that somewhere inside it has touched that person and it has strengthened your own vibration. Somewhere it has started a process of softening their dense energy. Send positive energy to difficult people and your good vibrations will dissolve some of their negativity.

I believe that the energy crisis on earth is actually a symbol of the energy crisis people around the planet are having within themselves. But as the world truly wakes up, and we become aware of our own energy, so the world situation will resolve. As we all begin to create a wonderful energy within and around ourselves and others, the earth will receive our vibration and it will help to make the world a better place.

Contacting the Authors

To contact Anne Jirsch, please email anne@annejirsch.com or visit her website at www.annejirsch.com where you can download guided visualisations that appear in this book.

To contact Monica Cafferky, please visit her website www.monicacafferky.com. For Monica's online yoga and meditation classes, visit www.verandayoga.com.

Appendix

Below are contact details for experts mentioned in the book, along with contact information for various practitioner organisations.

Masaru Emoto
For further details of Masaru Emoto's work, visit his website at www.masaruemoto.net

Professor Wiseman and the Luck Factor
For information on Professor Wiseman and his groundbreaking work, visit www.richardwiseman.com

Where to Go to Find a Practitioner

Acupuncture
The British Acupuncture Council
www.acupuncture.org.uk
Tel: 0208 735 0400

Alexander Technique
The Society of Teachers of the Alexander Technique
www.stat.org.uk
Tel: 020 7351 0828

Allergies
The British Allergy Foundation
www.allergyfoundation.com
Tel: 01322 619898

Bach Flower Remedies
The British Association of Flower Essence Producers
www.bafep.com
Tel: 01392 832005

Healers
The National Federation of Spiritual Teachers
www.nfsh.org.uk
Tel: 01932 783164
Bio energy healer Seka Nikolic can be contacted via
www.sekanikolic.com

Homeopathy
The British Homeopathic Association
www.trusthomeopathy.org
Tel: 0870 444 3950

Hypnotherapy
The Hypnotherapy Association
www.thehypnotherapyassociation.co.uk
Tel: 01257 262124

Kinesiology
The Association of Systematic Kinesiology (as.K)
www.kinesiology.co.uk
Tel: 020 8399 3215

Massage
The British Federation of Massage Practitioners
www.jolanta.co.uk
Tel: 01772 881063

Natural Hormone Treatments (Progesterone)
Health Science & Serenity
www.progesterone.org.uk
Tel: 01481 233 370

Neuro-Linguistic Programming (NLP)
The Professional Guild of NLP
www.professionalguildofnlp.com
Tel: 0845 2267334

Nutrition
The British Nutrition Foundation
www.nutrition.org.uk
Tel: 020 7404 6504

Thought Field Therapy
The British Thought Field Therapy Association
www.btfta.org
Tel: 0845 226 4812

Yoga
Find a teacher at Yoga Hub
www.yogahub.co.uk

The British Wheel of Yoga
www.bwy.org.uk
Tel: 015 293 06851

Bibliography

Anderson, M., *Numerology: The Secret Power of Numbers*, Aquarian Press, Northamptonshire, 1985

Allen, J., *As Man Thinketh*, Cosimo Classics, New York, 2005

Bruce, A., *Beyond the Bleep*, The Disinformation Company, New York, 2005

Callahan, R, J., *Tapping the Healer Within*, Contemporary Books, Chicago, 2001

Carnegie, A., *The Gospel of Wealth*, Penguin Classics, 2006

Carnegie, D., *How to Win Friends and Influence People*, Simon & Schuster, New York, 1998 (New Ed)

DeMohan, E., *The Harmonics of Sound, Color & Vibration*, De Vorss & Co, California, 1980

Dunstan, V., *How to Develop the Money Magnet in Your Mind*, Megiddo Press Ltd, Cardiff, 1984

Eason, C., *Pendulum Dowsing*, Piatkus, London, 1999

Fin, K., *Feng Shui*, Landsdowne Publishing, Australia, 1997

Freud, S., *The Interpretation of Dreams*, Kessinger Publishing Co, Montana, 2004

Gimbel, T., *The Colour Therapy Workbook*, Element, London, 1993

Godwin, J., *Music, Mysticism and Magic*, Arkana, London, 1986

Goldman, J., *Healing Sounds*, Healing Arts Press, Vermont, 2002

Hochswender, W., Martin, G., & Morino, T., *The Buddha in Your Mirror*, Middleway Press, California, 2001

Holbeche, S., *The Power of Gems and Crystals*, Piatkus, London, 1992

Jirsch, A., *Instant Intuition*, Piatkus, London, 2007

Jirsch, A., *The Future Is Yours*, Piatkus, London, 2007

Jones, A., *Healing Negative Energies*, Piatkus, London, 2002

Kenton, L., *The X Factor Diet*, Vermilion, London, 2002

Kerrell, B., and Goggin, K., *The Guide to Pyramid Power*, Forces Publishing, Santa Monica, 1975

Keyes, K., *The Hundredth Monkey Effect*, De Vorss & Co, California, 1984

Kingston, K., *Creating Sacred Space with Feng Shui*, Piatkus, London, 1996

Laszlo, E., *Science and the Akashic Field*, Inner Traditions, Vermont, 2007

Lubeck, W., *Pendulum Healing Handbook*, New Age Books, 2000

Markham, U., *Fortune Telling by Crystals*, Aquarian Press, 1987

McKenna, P., *I Can Make You Rich*, Bantam, London, 2007

McTaggart, L., *The Field*, Element, London, 2003

Mullis, K., *Dancing Naked in the Mind Field*, Vintage Books, New York, 1998

Muramoto, N., and Abehsera, M., *Healing Ourselves*, Michael Dempsey Press, London, 1975

Nielsen G., and Polansky, J., *Pendulum Power*, Inner Traditions, New York, 1977

Parnia, S., *What Happens When We Die?*, Hay House, California, 2008

Playfair, G., *Twin Telepathy*, Sterling Publishing. New York, 2002

Radin, D., *Entangled Minds*, Paraview, New York, 2006

Radin, D., *The Conscious Universe*, Harper Edge, San Francisco, 1997

Rael, J., *Being and Vibration*, Council Oak Books, LLC, Oklahoma, 1993

Ryan Hyde, C., *Pay It Forward*, Simon & Schuster, New York, 2000

Sheldrake, R., *A New Science of Life*, Park Street Press, Vermont, 1995

Sheldrake, R., *The Sense of Being Stared At*, Random House, London, 2003

Too, L., *128 Tips for Wealth and Prosperity*, Oriental Publications, 2000

Too, L., *How to Make Your First Million*, Random House, London, 2000

Toth, M., and Nielsen, G., *Pyramid Power*, Excalibur Books, Northamptonshire, England, 1981

Watson, L., *Supernature*, Coronet Books, London, 1973

Watson et al, *Selected Writings of Nichiren*, Burton, Columbia University Press, 1990

Wilde, S., *The Trick to Money is Having Some*, Hay House, California, 1995

Wiseman, R. *The Luck Factor*, Arrow, London, 2004

Index

Note: Page numbers in **bold** refer to diagrams.